Religious Fundamentalism and Social Identity

D0144121

The attacks on the World Trade Center and the Pentagon of September 11th, 2001 brought the phenomenon of religious fundamentalism to the world's attention. Sociological research has clearly demonstrated that fundamentalists are primarily reacting against modernity, and believe that they are fighting for the very survival of their faith against the secular enemy. But we understand very little about how and why people join fundamentalist movements and embrace a set of beliefs, values and norms of behaviour which are counter-cultural. This is essentially a question for social psychology, since it involves both social relations and individual selves.

Drawing on a broad theoretical perspective, social identity theory, Peter Herriot addresses two key questions: why do fundamentalists identify themselves as an in-group fighting against various out-groups? And how do the psychological needs for self-esteem and meaning motivate them? Case studies of Mohammed Atta, the leader of the 9/11 hijackers, and of the current controversy in the Anglican Church about gay priests and bishops, demonstrate how fruitfully this theory can be applied to fundamentalist conflicts. It also offers psychologically sensible ways of managing such conflicts, rather than treating fundamentalists as an enemy to be defeated.

Religious Fundamentalism and Social Identity is unique in applying social identity theory to fundamentalism, and rare in that it provides psychological (in addition to sociological) analyses of the phenomenon. It is a valuable resource for courses in social psychology which seek to demonstrate the applicability of social psychological theory to the real world.

Religious Fundamentalism and Social Identity

Peter Herriot

Routledge
Taylor & Francis Group

LONDON AND NEW YORK

First published 2007 by Routledge
27 Church Road, Hove, East Sussex BN3 2FA

Simultaneously published in the USA and Canada
by Routledge
270 Madison Avenue, New York, NY 10016

Routledge is an imprint of the Taylor & Francis Group, an informa business

Copyright © 2007 Psychology Press

Typeset in Times by Garfield Morgan, Swansea, West Glamorgan
Printed and bound in Great Britain by TJ International Ltd, Padstow,
Cornwall
Cover design by Design Deluxe, Bath

British Library Cataloguing in Publication Data
A catalogue record for this book is available from the British Library

Library of Congress Cataloging-in-Publication Data
Herriot, Peter.
  Religious fundamentalism and social identity / Peter Herriot.
       p. cm.
  Includes bibliographical references and index.
  ISBN 13: 978-0-415-41676-4 (hardback)
  ISBN 10: 0-415-41676-0 (hardback)
  ISBN 13: 978-0-415-41677-1 (pbk.)
  ISBN 10: 0-415-41677-9 (pbk.)
1. Religious fundamentalism. 2. Group identity. I. Title.
  BL238 H47 2007
  306.6–dc22
                                                        2006022742

ISBN 978-0-415-41676-4 (hbk)
ISBN 978-0-415-41677-1 (pbk)

Contents

Introduction

The assault on the World Trade Center and the Pentagon on September 11th 2001 (hereafter '9/11') had many profound consequences. One of the more important was that it forced western elites to recognise the existence of fundamentalist religion and its importance to the future of the world. Hitherto, fundamentalism, if it had been noticed at all, was popularly considered to be one of the primitive peculiarities of impoverished countries in the developing world. Now it suddenly appeared as a mysterious threat to us all.

While 9/11 forced the world to recognise the existence of religious fundamentalism, it also resulted in some false assumptions about its nature. The first such misconception is that *fundamentalism is necessarily associated with violence*. By far the majority of fundamentalists disagree profoundly with the use of terrorist tactics (defined as the intentional use of violence against civilians); many sympathise with the aims of the terrorists while disapproving of their means; a very few engage in violent action. For example, it is arguable that the majority of the 40–50 per cent of Americans who describe themselves as 'born-again Christians'[1] are fundamentalists (in terms of the definition provided in Chapter 1). Very few of them contemplate the use of any violence which is not sanctioned by the state. It is indeed an important question as to why some fundamentalists act violently;[2] but violence is certainly not a defining characteristic of fundamentalism.

The second misconception follows from the first. It argues that, because it is violent in nature, *fundamentalism cannot really be genuinely religious*; it must be some sort of aberration. It is true that the mainstream versions of the major world religions are hostile to violence except in exceptional circumstances for defensive purposes. But it is also true that, historically, adherents of mainstream religions have frequently engaged in violent activities for religious reasons.[3] Thus not only is fundamentalism not necessarily violent in nature, but mainstream religion often has been. Hence it is impossible to treat fundamentalism as an entirely separate phenomenon from ordinary religion. On the contrary, fundamentalists form a considerable and growing part of each of the major world religions. It is arguable that Islam, Judaism, Hinduism and Christianity are each divided between fundamentalists on the one hand, and a more liberal mainstream on the other. Thus the common belief that religion was merely a post hoc justification for 9/11 is mistaken. A particularly extreme form of fundamentalist religion motivated that action.

Few still believe that fundamentalism is solely an Islamic phenomenon. But many appear to labour under a related misconception, that *it is a throwback to the premodern or medieval era*, typical of poorer rural societies. Nothing could be further from the truth. Fundamentalism is essentially a modern social movement of the twentiety century (or rather, to be accurate, *fundamentalisms* are twentieth-century phenomena, since many social movements arose during that period in different societal contexts which may each be described as religious fundamentalism). Fundamentalists represent themselves as returning to the pure premodern origins of their faith, as prescribed by their sacred books and as practised by their legendary founders and heroes. In fact, however, they use modern means to battle against modernity, and arguably are frequently operating at a postmodern level of sophistication in their use of the media.[4] Moreover, their attempts to justify their holy book in analytical, historical and scientific terms, rather than treating it as a source of spiritually inspiring myths, is a product of their own modernism.[5]

In reaction to the modern attempt to disentangle religion from politics and treat it as a private and individual activity, fundamentalists have sought to blur the distinction between the sacred and the secular, and instead to transform the secular entirely into the sacred. This, of course, is the reverse of what they perceive to be the current situation: for them, the secular is overwhelming the sacred. The view of fundamentalists as constituting political blocs and pushing through a political agenda has recently been reinforced by the re-election of President George W. Bush. His success was attributed in large part to the mobilisation of the fundamentalist vote. Subsequent polls indicated that some 22 per cent of

the electorate rated 'moral' issues such as abortion and gay marriage as the most important determinant of their vote.[6]

However, this perception of *fundamentalists as being actively
engaged in the political process* is partial at best. Many of them
come to recognise that politics is the art of the possible, and that
compromise is an essential element in political success. This is alien
to their absolutist beliefs. Second, their success in achieving their
political aims has not hitherto been great. For example, very few
Arab states have operated according to pure Islamic political and
legal principles, while attempts to reverse American legislation on
abortion, divorce and minority rights have largely failed. As a
result, such failed political activity has frequently been succeeded
by two opposite reactions: some fundamentalists have withdrawn
into their enclaves, and become politically involved only in order to
secure their rights to practise their religion; or sometimes, they
have turned to violence.[7]

Another misconception about fundamentalists is that *the content
of what they believe is so bizarre as to be unworthy of our consideration*. Their beliefs, values and norms of behaviour do indeed appear
utterly foreign to modern sensibilities. They seem to be derived
from an entirely different worldview to our own. But unless we
grasp the nature of that worldview, we cannot hope to understand
the social movements which fundamentalists represent, nor the
activities in which they engage. It is not sufficient to recognise that
they are reacting against modernity and secularism. We also need
to explore their views of history and the future, their beliefs about
God and their attribution of authority. For example, we cannot
properly understand the support of fundamentalist American
Christians for the state of Israel unless we are familiar with their
prophetic beliefs.[8]

All of these popular misconceptions following 9/11 derive from a
lack of familiarity with the research which has already been carried
out on fundamentalisms. This work has indicated to the satisfaction of most scholars that there does exist a family resemblance
among a large group of religiously-based social movements worldwide. Further, it has specified the defining characteristics which
distinguish this category from other religious and social movements.[9] It has also been generally agreed that the term 'fundamentalism' is worth using to label the category. This is despite its
original usage as referring specifically to some American Protestants in the 1920s, who stood firm for five fundamental beliefs of the

faith which needed to be defended against liberal theologians. It is also despite its more general use in recent times to refer to any religious group of which one disapproves.

This book therefore starts in Chapter 1 by describing the ground-breaking work of sociologists in defining fundamentalism in terms of its distinctive characteristics. I seek to demonstrate how the five defining features of fundamentalism derive from its reaction against secular modernity, and how these features are interrelated. In Chapter 2, I argue that a social psychological perspective is likely to provide additional understanding of fundamentalism as a phenomenon. Social psychology is the discipline which provides the essential link between social movements and their individual adherents. I outline social identity theory as providing the most useful overall explanatory framework presently available. The predictions derived from social identity theory have not been empirically tested as yet, but in Chapter 3 I review psychological evidence which at least is not inconsistent with these predictions. In order to provide further empirical support, in Chapters 4 and 5 I present two case studies of fundamentalist conflicts. The first uses the story of Mohammed Atta, the leader of the 9/11 hijackers, to demonstrate that they were inspired by militant fundamentalism. The second reviews the current dispute in the Anglican Communion regarding gay priests and bishops, and shows that this too is basically a fundamentalist conflict. Chapter 6 argues that social identity theory provides a coherent explanatory account of these two conflicts, albeit a post hoc one. Finally, in Chapter 7, I assert the possibility that social identity theory also provides a rationale for managing these and other fundamentalist conflicts.

Thus the book seeks to address the psychological issue which remains largely unaddressed in published analyses of fundamentalisms (but see Note 10). These are mostly concerned with the sociological analysis of fundamentalisms as social movements. The psychological issue is: how do these social movements exercise their power over the beliefs, values and behaviour of their adherents? What, in other words, is the relationship between the social movements, together with the groups of which they are composed, and the individual selves of their members? It is generally accepted that fundamentalists are not suffering from a psychological pathology, nor can they reliably be distinguished from the rest of humanity by specific characteristics of personality. The answer to this question therefore has to be located in a theory of why individuals join and stay with groups; how group membership impacts upon individuals; and how that impact affects beliefs, values and norms of behaviour. If this book is to succeed, it will have to demonstrate the capability of social identity theory to provide that explanation.

The aim of this book is definitely not reductionist, however. I do not seek to 'explain away' religious experience in psychological terms, nor do I wish to supplant the perspectives which scholars from other disciplines, such as history, sociology, theology and philosophy, bring to the study of fundamentalisms. I merely want to add a psychological perspective, which may help to increase the understanding of one of the most urgent issues of our times. At the same time, however, I would like to demonstrate to students of psychology that the theories which they learn so laboriously from textbooks can have real practical application for the understanding and management of social and political issues.

Chapter 1

Fundamentalism versus secularism

Fundamentalism defined

The term fundamentalism 'refers to a discernible pattern of religious militance by which self-styled "true believers" attempt to arrest the erosion of religious identity, fortify the borders of the religious community, and create viable alternatives to secular institutions and behaviors'.[1] This definition encapsulates the conclusions of the most broad-ranging research project yet conducted on the nature of fundamentalism, the Fundamentalism Project at the University of Chicago.

The investigators established, to their own satisfaction and that of most other scholars, that it is justifiable to refer to fundamentalism as a general category which subsumes a large number of specific religious movements across the world. The term is not used to refer only to the specific Protestant religious movement in America, which gave itself the label fundamentalist in the 1920s. In order to come to such a conclusion, the Chicago investigators needed to confirm that there were features which distinguished these movements from other religious and secular social movements. They concluded that there were five such features, the most important of which is *reactivity*: hostility to the secular modern world. From this basic feature follow four others: *dualism*, the tendency to evaluate in starkly binary terms, as good or bad; *authority*, the willingness to believe and obey the sacred book of the movement and/or its leaders; *selectivity*, the choice, from the sacred book or the movement's tradition, of certain beliefs and practices in preference to others; and *millennialism*, the belief that God will triumph in the end and establish his kingdom on earth. Scholars have differed in the importance which they attach to each of these criteria, but all or most feature in the majority of their definitions.

Some fundamentalist movements are overwhelmingly religious in orientation, but in others the religious element is strongly associated with nationalist and/or ethnic features. For example, Muslim fundamentalist movements are generally strongly pro-Arab and anti-imperialist in tone. It is this latter type of fundamentalist movement which is more likely to engage in violent activity.[2] Not all fundamentalisms exhibit all of the five definitive features strongly. Of the 18 movements investigated in the research, only 4 demonstrated all five features to a high degree. These were American Protestants, Shi'ite Muslims, and Haredi and Gush Emunim Jews. A further 8 showed four features to a high degree.[3] The identity of these four most fundamentalist of the fundamentalisms is not accidental. They are all based upon the three major Abrahamic religions: Judaism, Islam and Christianity. All three have ancient traditions, considering the patriarch Abraham to have been in some sense a founder of their faith. Likewise, all three are 'religions of the book', placing great emphasis upon their holy book as a source of belief and practice. Thus they all provide a clear opportunity to fundamentalists to criticise the apostasy of those who have fallen away from the pure and simple origins of the ancient faith; and to select their favoured beliefs and practices from the holy book, thereby conferring authority upon them.

The central and defining feature of fundamentalism is *reactivity against modernism*. Modernism is defined as the set of secular values and beliefs derived from modernity (the organisational and technological developments which underpin modern societies). Fundamentalists perceive modernism, and the secular societies which express it, as being hostile to their religion and intent on destroying it: 'This defence of religion is the sine qua non of fundamentalism; without it, a movement may not properly be termed fundamentalist'.[4] If fundamentalism is to be construed as a modern reaction against modernism, we would expect fundamentalisms to come into existence after the effects of modernism become apparent.[5] This does in fact appear to be the case. The first nation to modernise was the USA, and fundamentalism first appeared there (and, indeed, acquired its name) in the 1920s. The state of Israel became a modern secular state in 1945. The most dreadful outcome of rational bureaucratic modernity, the Holocaust, had just occurred. Jewish fundamentalisms started appearing soon afterwards. Islamic fundamentalisms were the last to appear, in the 1960s and 1970s, probably because secular regimes in such Muslim countries as Iran and Egypt had been relatively recently established.

The struggles of fundamentalisms with modernism are initially primarily conducted within, rather than between, societies. The contending parties are initially the fundamentalists and those whom they feel to be their most dangerous foes: religious people who have allowed secular beliefs, values and norms of behaviour (hereafter 'BVNs') to corrupt the pure faith – apostates, all of them. Next come other representatives of secularism: for example, the media, liberals of all persuasions and perhaps the state itself. Once again, the evidence by and large supports this implication. Most fundamentalist movements have vented their initial hostility upon liberal adherents of their parent religion. Thus for example, American Protestant fundamentalists initially attacked liberal theology and the reworking of the biblical creation myth to accord with evolutionary science.[6] Later they attacked societal targets such as the feminist and gay movements.[7] Militant Islamic fundamentalists initially targeted lukewarm Muslims and nominally Muslim regimes such as Egypt and Iran. More recently they have turned their attention to infidels in general and the Great Satan, America, in particular.[8]

The initial identification of mainstream liberal believers as the main enemy is today reflected throughout the world's religions. Strong fundamentalist movements are to be found, not only in all the major world religions, but also within the different forms or denominations of those religions. For example, all of the Christian denominations, except those which were fundamentalist from the start, have recently been riven by strife largely created by fundamentalist believers. Even the Anglican Church, historically a pillar of tolerance and diversity, is on the brink of schism (see Chapter 5). The fundamentalists are absolutely correct: the basic difference is that more liberal believers do not treat the secular world as their enemy. On the contrary, they see God at work in many of the features of modernity, and happily use the intellectual tools which derive from the Enlightenment in their belief and practice. Indeed, the original coinage of the term 'fundamentalism' was the result of liberal Christians using modern methods of textual analysis in their study of the Bible.

Thus the gulf between fundamentalist and liberal believers is indeed immense. It is manifest in the traditional liberal dilemma:

do I exercise my liberal tolerance even towards those who do not tolerate me? But most important of all, the basic definitive characteristic of fundamentalisms, that they are a reaction against the secular world, is not shared by the more liberal mainstreams. As I will seek to show, this reactivity is central to any attempt to explain fundamentalism in psychological terms, for it constitutes an opportunity for the 'us versus them' dynamic which underpins social conflict.

Thus, historically, fundamentalisms have struggled with the mainstreams of their own religious denominations, and with the immediate secular culture in which they were located. These struggles have been localised in nature throughout most of the twentieth century. However, with the increase in the globalisation of communications and cultures, such struggles have lately become worldwide in their scope. For example, at first glance the internecine struggle of the Anglican Church over the ordination of gays, which constitutes the case study in Chapter 5, is a local religious quarrel. However, even this apparently parochial dispute is in fact global in scale. Fundamentalist African bishops have played a major role, and the fundamentalist side is supported by funds from a wealthy American conservative[9] and by a powerful American pressure group, the Institute on Research and Democracy. Globalised communications facilitated global politicisation of the issues.

As for my first case study, concerning the leader of the 9/11 hijackers Mohammed Atta (Chapter 4), the global dimension of that struggle is evident from Osama bin Laden's target, and from President Bush's responsive 'war on terror'. The very language of the conflict is expressed in apocalyptic cosmic terminology, with the forces of the 'axis of evil' being ranged against 'the Great Satan'. Furthermore, the struggle is being fought out as much in the global media as it is on the ground.

These two very different twenty-first-century cases illustrate the recent increasing globalisation of fundamentalisms. However, the essence of the fundamentalist phenomenon remains the same. It is a reaction against modernism, whether that reaction is conducted on a local or a global stage. The struggle is between 'strong religion'[10] and modernism, not between different religions.

However, the major opposing theory of religious conflict argues, on the contrary, that such conflicts represent a clash of civilisations.[11] Samuel Huntington proposes that globalisation has rendered the world's eight major civilisations more obvious and known to each other. At the same time it has caused individuals to reaffirm their civilisational identities as Sinic, Japanese, Indian, Islamic, Western, Orthodox, Latin American, or African. Civilisations are differentiated by their respective cultures, and the most profound feature of many of these cultures is their religion. Huntington argues that the upsurge in membership of the world's major religions in the last quarter of the twentieth century is evidence of the increasing importance of civilisational identities. He locates recent and current conflicts at the geographical fault lines between civilisations (for example, in the Balkans). Analysing these conflicts in more detail, he concludes that of 28 conflicts between Muslims and others, 19 were between the Muslim and Christian civilisations. He attributes these conflicts to a variety of causal factors, but prime among them he cites the growing hostility of Muslims *in general* to the West and its secularism.

Thus there are two very different views of the role of religion in conflicts. Huntington perceives religions *as a whole* as representative of conflicted civilisational cultures. Others[12,13] disagree. First, they argue that Huntington's thesis overemphasises the commonalities within civilisations. They doubt that civilisational cultures are uniform, and that civilisational identities are of particular importance to many of the world's inhabitants. Second, they believe that fundamentalisms, rather than entire religions, are by their very nature conflictual and fuel religious conflicts. In their view, these struggles may be merely institutional (within the religion), they may involve political involvement of a peaceful nature or they may become violent conflicts within or between nation states.

Huntington's thesis, on the other hand, denies the very basis of this argument: that there exist fundamentalist movements in every major religion, which are very different from the mainstream of that religion and deeply hostile to it. This clash, it is argued, is within cultures, rather than between them. It initially takes the form of a struggle within a religion, because the mainstream form of that religion has embraced various elements of modernism, whereas the fundamentalists claim to reject modernism in its entirety. Thus those issues over which within-religion conflicts are fought relate to secular BVNs which the mainstream has incorporated. This is why these battles concern such issues as sexual morality and women's roles. These issues represent some of the important values of modernism regarding the rights of individuals and the recognition of the pluralist nature of modern societies.

Historically, these conflicts have been conducted within religions, but more recently they have also occurred between fundamentalists and non-religious secularists. Thus I return to the basic proposition: that fundamentalisms are reactions against modernism wherever they occur – locally, nationally, or globally. The conflict is between different ideologies, not between civilisations, as Huntington would have it. The fundamentalist worldview is absolutist, both in terms of individual belief and also with respect to society. Many fundamentalists would like everyone to be like them, preferably under theocratic rule. Non-fundamentalists mostly recognise that they live in a pluralist society, and that other people hold different beliefs and values, to which they are entitled.

Who is the enemy?

However, while it is possible to define and describe fundamentalism with a degree of confidence, the same cannot be said for modernism as its enemy. There is some agreement about how secular modernism may be described from a scholarly and analytic perspective.[14] But things become much more difficult when we seek to discover the nature of the fundamentalists' enemy. For there are certain features of modernity, and to a lesser extent of modernism, which fundamentalists embrace wholeheartedly.

First, as already noted (see p. 8), fundamentalists cannot help being intellectual children of their time. They fall, perhaps unawares, into modern modes of thought. For example, they are particularly given to a factual, empirical, historical and literalist frame of mind. This perspective is perhaps also derived from the practical technological bent of many of the more educated fundamentalists. Mohammed Atta was an engineer by training, as were a considerable proportion of the leaders of the American fundamentalist churches.[15] The result is a belief system which refuses to recognise the nature and purpose of myth.[16] Myths are stories which speak to people's deepest spiritual and psychological needs. Instead, some fundamentalists try to apply supposedly scientific criteria of truth to all aspects of their belief, particularly those derived from the holy book. So, for example, American fundamentalists have developed a 'scientific' creationism in defence of the account of creation in the book of Genesis.[17] Scientific creationism is a contradiction in terms; it is trying to turn a myth into a historical and scientific account. They also believe in the literal physical resurrection and ascension into heaven of Christ, and expect Him to return to earth in a similar way.[18] Ironically, by espousing a 'scientific' approach they have brought down the hostility of many scientists upon themselves, although such opposition only convinces them more strongly that they are right.

Muslim and Jewish fundamentalists, too, are partly modern in their belief systems. Following the example of such modern social movements as communism, they create tightly constructed and internally consistent ideologies based on selective elements of the mainstream faith.[19] The writings of the radical Muslim clerics, Mawdudi and Qutb (see pp. 65–72), are notable for the internal consistency of their turgidly written arguments. As with Christian fundamentalism, once the initial assumptions are granted, the ideology is worked out with a thoroughly modern logic.

A second aspect of modernity which has been embraced by fundamentalists is the marketing emphasis of modern consumerism.[20] In America this has been developed into a highly sophisticated process. The traditional underlying fundamentalist beliefs about a God who intervenes supernaturally, Christ's atoning death, physical resurrection, and his imminent return to earth and the inerrancy of the Word of God, the Bible, through which he speaks directly to the individual, are all retained intact. But the attraction and retention of adherents has been supported by segmented marketing of considerable skill. A wide variety of demographic groups is targeted with sophisticated techniques, and individualised website interactions are provided to help with frequently presenting problems.[21] The tools of the 'therapy industry' are employed in God's name.

Militant Muslims, on the other hand, use other people's media to promote their cause. News media around the world carry accounts and pictures of violent crimes which are committed in order to send a message of fear. The deeds of Osama bin Laden, of suicide bombers in Israel and of kidnappers in Iraq tell the world that it is not safe from a vengeful God and his faithful servants.[22] The other major free global organ, the internet, contains much Islamic recruitment material. For example, a dedicated youth site offers an apologia for the radical cleric Sayyid Qutb, together with the text of his most famous book.[23]

Similarly, fundamentalists have become adept at using modern political techniques of organisation and communication. In their efforts to take over the Anglican Church, fundamentalists'

organisation at the crucial Lambeth Conference of 1998 was said
to resemble that of an American political party at election time.[24]
The American 'moral majority' actually did so organise in the
1980s, putting up a presidential candidate in Pat Robertson.[25] They
have proved themselves second to none in their organisation at
grass roots level, for example taking over school boards and party
caucuses.[26] Meanwhile, Jewish fundamentalists continuously play
skilful political games as they jockey for control of the right wing
of the Israeli Knesset.

Many of the features of modernity have given rise to the conditions in which fundamentalisms flourish.[27] For example, the
segmentation of modern life into many different arenas for action
has for many led to a fragmentation of their experience and a
feeling of alienation and insecurity. Likewise, industrialisation has
resulted in urbanisation and the creation of an urban proletariat
uprooted from their rural origins. People feel they have little
control over what happens to them, and cannot foresee what the
future may hold. In such conditions, any social movement which
offers membership, self-esteem, meaning and purpose can flourish.
Fundamentalisms have certainly not identified these aspects of
modernity as their enemy, however, perhaps wisely in so far as they
are a necessary condition for fundamentalisms' growth. Rather,
they have targeted those aspects of secularism which more directly
challenge their BVNs.

Their most basic belief is that there is only one correct set of
BVNs, and that is their own. Hence societal pluralism, personal
individualism, moral relativism and political liberalism are their
real cultural enemies. The Enlightenment notion of human beings
as rational creatures in charge of their own destiny underpins such
values. However, these abstractions are not sufficiently concrete
foes against which to rally the troops. It is easier to mobilise action
against groups which clearly violate fundamentalist values. So, for
example, the high value placed on the traditional patriarchal family
by all fundamentalisms has been violated in America by the success
of a variety of interest groups, such as feminists and gays, in
securing their individual rights. It is these groups, and the legislation which supports their rights, which have been selected as the
prime target.

Fundamentalist Muslims, meanwhile, can broadly blame the
Great Satan for a general cultural imperialism which spreads such
heresy across the globe, both in the media and by imitation in

secularised Arab states. As for Jewish extremists, they concentrate their rage against secular Zionists, insufficiently religious Jews, and Arabs, all of whom fail to obey the Torah and are a threat to the gaining of Eretz Israel, the land God gave to his people by his promise to Abraham.[28]

Martial metaphors are to be found in the mainstream forms of all of the world's major religions. 'Onward Christian soldiers' has its parallels everywhere else. What makes fundamentalisms unique is their belief that their religion is under threat of extinction by the forces of modernism. Such fear for their survival leads them very naturally to the use of the war metaphor. There is the imminent possibility of personal humiliation if their religion, with which they identify strongly, is destroyed. American fundamentalists suffered humiliation at the hands of the scientific and liberal establishment at the Scopes 'monkey trial' of the teaching of evolutionary theory in public school in the 1920s. As a consequence they withdrew into their laager, became politically right wing, and created a tight and controlled network of organisations in order better to fight the good fight.[29] Radical Muslims were repeatedly humiliated by the secular leaders of their nations, who imprisoned and executed their respected leaders. In fear for their survival, and having failed to foment revolution in their own countries, they declared war on the Great Satan itself. Fear so profound is likely to lead to aggression. There can be only one winner in such a fight to the death, they believe, so no compromise is possible. They are soldiers in a cosmic war.

On the other hand, fundamentalists' relationship with the secular world is symbiotic. They would fail to exist at all if there were no secular world to fight against, since the struggle is their *raison d'être*. Hence, paradoxically, they cannot afford to win. As Mark Juergensmeyer observes, 'one cannot have a war without an enemy'.[30]

Not only do fundamentalists depend for their very existence on an enemy, they also derive from their role as cosmic warriors a purpose for their lives (to fight the good fight), a way of making sense of the world (as a constant struggle), and an inspiring vision of the future (God will win in the end, however bad things look at present). Furthermore, the martial metaphor offers the violent few a justification for their actions. After all, in war the usual rules no longer apply. We have to do what we have to do to win. Reverend Michael Bray justified his assaults on American abortion clinics as simply constituting a preliminary skirmish in the culture war.[31] Terrorist attacks in which many civilians are killed are entirely justified, since these victims are not perceived as people but rather as representatives of the secular world. Dehumanising the enemy is a staple technique to persuade the troops to kill them. By breaking social rules in these ways, fundamentalists can also give themselves a feeling of power. No longer are they in danger of humiliation. Rather, they are God's agents, acting according to His rules, and changing the course of history on His behalf. They are signalling that religion is still a force to be reckoned with.

Now of course, most fundamentalists use the analogy of war in a metaphorical sense only. They do not advocate or use physical violence to defend their faith. However, we may legitimately ask what it is which turns a few of these deeply pious and religious people, who are often noted for their personal kindness and charity, into terrorists.[32] We may address this question at two levels of analysis, the societal and the personal. From the societal perspective, it is not difficult to understand why it is that fundamentalist movements which have been persecuted by the state, and whose leaders have been imprisoned and executed, are more likely to use violence. And given the overwhelmingly superior military forces of the state, it is hardly surprising that fundamentalist violence takes the form of terrorism. They would stand no chance in a conventional war, as the recent invasion of Afghanistan demonstrated. Only by inducing terror, they believe, can they persuade the secular world that there is indeed a cosmic war going on and that, despite appearances to the contrary, they still retain some power.

The question as to why fundamentalism turns violent at the individual level of analysis is more interesting from a psychological perspective, however. Indeed, it is a question which is subsumed under a more general issue: how can a social movement such as a fundamentalism persuade its members to believe dogmas, hold values and carry out actions which are counter-cultural? This is the issue to which this book is primarily addressed. But, to return to the more particular question, why is a person who suffers from no obvious psychological dysfunction prepared to kill for their cause?

There is a set of theoretical explanations relating to group membership and identity which I will describe fully in Chapter 2. At this point, it is worth stressing the importance of the dualistic fundamentalist belief system. The foe is the secular world, that is, everyone other than oneself and one's fellow fundamentalists. The duality is therefore between 'us' (God's soldiers) and 'them' (His enemies). There is a vast chasm between the two worldviews held by us and them, constituting entirely different, and usually opposite, BVNs. The choice of a vast and varied enemy, modernism, results in the depersonalisation of 'them'. Individuals are merely examples of the enemy, all to be treated the same. And God's rules permit, nay require, violent assault on the secular world. It will become absolutely clear in Chapter 4 that the 9/11 hijackers believed that, as was their duty, they were doing God's will. Violent fundamentalists are simply acting on the basis of their worldview.

If that belief system is literalist in its view of the sacred book, or if it has never distinguished clearly between the spiritual and the temporal realms of discourse, then it is easy to put a violent meaning and intent onto a spiritually intended message. Finally, if the belief system emphasises that we are in the last days and that apocalypse is near, then it justifies desperate measures to aid the divine purpose and hasten the divine timetable.

Dualism, authority, selectivity and millennialism

The issue of fundamentalist violence understandably preoccupies us at this present historical moment. However, the more basic task is to understand fundamentalisms in general. Whether or not they express their reaction to secularism violently, the basic question is how their hostility to the modern world has come to dominate their religious movement and their individual BVNs. The second distinctive feature of fundamentalisms, the essentially dualist nature of their belief systems, adds to our understanding.

Dualism refers to fundamentalists' tendency to perceive and evaluate reality in terms of binary opposites.[33] Needless to say, the favourable alternative always applies to themselves. Given the importance of correct doctrine to fundamentalists, it is not surprising that truth versus error (or falsehood) features prominently in their discourse. This distinction is very useful, in so far as it justifies hostility towards those in theological error, that is to say, the mainstream adherents of their religion. More general distinctions, for example, the faith versus the world, or spiritual versus carnal (or material), permit secular values to be targeted. The yet more general distinction, good versus evil, can be personified as

God versus the Devil, and used to justify the selection of any enemy and their demonisation and dehumanisation.

Dualism is therefore an extremely useful adjunct to the war metaphor. First, it provides a flexible conceptual framework into which fundamentalists can slot any specific current enemy whom they wish to attack. Second, it helps to unify the faithful to form a bastion against the godless and the apostate, a strong 'us' against a godless 'them', the light shining in the darkness. Common beliefs and ideology are a powerful social cement. Finally, dualism is also a very helpful source of clarity and meaning for individuals who cannot tolerate the many shades of grey in a complex world. It helps to sort things out in one's mind if right is right and wrong is wrong; if men are men and women are women;[34] if truth is divine and error human; if God is responsible for the good things that happen in life, and Satan for the bad ones. Above all, it gives supernatural justification for hoping and working for a new social order.

However, the question remains. How has the individual fundamentalist believer come to perceive their religion as a war between two clearly defined enemies? Why is a counter-cultural worldview so compelling for so many? The importance of each fundamentalist movement's core BVNs in this regard cannot be exaggerated. Sharing the same BVNs gives tremendous cohesion. Members can congratulate each other that they are right and everyone else is wrong. They can recognise a fellow believer from what they say and how they say it, how they behave or even what they wear. They can, by the same token, distinguish themselves from all other groups. The more anti-secular and peculiar their BVNs, the more distinctive their group becomes. The unusual dress and behavioural rituals of the Haredi Jews mark them out from other not-so-pious but still religious Jews. What is more, to have engaged in such behaviour when it is so counter-cultural binds the new member in more tightly. 'I've done it, so it must be the right thing to do', runs the post hoc self-justification.[35]

However, probably the most important function of BVNs is to motivate action. Once BVNs have become internalised and are part of the member's identity, there is little need for external promises of reward or threats of punishment. Members are self-motivated. Therefore control of the nature and content of the BVNs is a crucial lever of power for leaders of fundamentalist movements. Fundamentalist ideology, particularly in the three 'religions of the book', claims that the holy book is the inerrant source of BVNs, interpreted by those inspired by God to do so. The belief that the holy book is the word of God forms the central plank of the creed of some fundamentalists. For example, *The Chicago Statement on Biblical Inerrancy* reads as follows:

> Holy Scripture, being God's own Word, written by men prepared and superintended by His Spirit, is of infallible divine authority in all matters upon which it touches: It is to be believed, as God's instruction, in all that it affirms; obeyed, as God's command, in all that it requires; embraced, as God's pledge, in all that it promises . . . Being wholly and verbally God-given, Scripture is without error or fault in all its teaching, no less in what it states about God's acts in creation, about the events of world history, and about its own literary origins under God, than in its witness to God's saving grace in individual lives.

Protestant fundamentalists do not necessarily believe in the literal truth of the Bible, since they recognise that it contains poetic language which includes various figures of speech. However, they insist that it is infallible, inerrant and internally consistent.[36]

Indeed, a recent text on the psychology of fundamentalism argues that belief in the holy book is the definitive characteristic of fundamentalism.[37] Ralph Hood and colleagues propose a model of 'intratextuality', which puts the holy text at centre stage as the source of the specific worldview held by the fundamentalism in question. As the reformed theologian Cornelius Van Til puts it, 'The Bible is thought of as authoritative on everything of which it speaks. And it speaks of everything'.[38] The fundamentalist's worldview is totally contained within the holy book, which therefore constitutes a self-contained meaning system. Any truth claim based on evidence or ideas from outside the holy book is subordinate to its authority. Liberal theologians, and non-fundamentalist Christians in general, are *inter*textualists: that is, they allow other sources than the Bible to have legitimate claims to truth. Therefore, in order to understand fundamentalists' worldview, argues Hood, we need to uncover the nature of their holy text and their engagement with it. In particular, we need to see how they succeed in making an internally consistent narrative out of its disparate contents.

However, the whole story is not simply to be found in the book itself and the believer's engagement with it. The BVNs held by fundamentalist groups are not read straight from its text. They are rather the result of highly partial *selection* and interpretation of parts of that text by fundamentalist leaders. The ideal of a pure and ancient tradition conceals a modern selective interpretation of textual material. As Gabriel Almond and colleagues say, 'the religious identity of the community . . . is always a construction of the sacred past from among a myriad of possibilities'.[39] Leaders have understood that to direct the faithful to take the desired action, they must first control the BVNs which motivate that action. So, for example, the Ayatollah Khomeini reinterpreted the role of mullahs so as to become not merely religious authorities but also political rulers. This justified his mobilisation of the faithful in his successful bid for power in Iran. Sayyed Qutb reinterpreted the doctrine of *jihad* radically in order to justify armed aggression in Egypt. In the 1980s Billy Graham adapted the dominant pre-millennialist eschatology, which stated that the second coming of Christ was fore-ordained and therefore it was pointless to engage in political activity. He needed to give the Protestant evangelicals a good reason for joining the moral majority's political crusade, so he argued that they could perhaps hasten the millennium along a little. Rabbi Kahane, who founded the Kach fundamentalist movement, changed the doctrine of spiritual separateness achieved by religious rituals to mean physical separateness from Arabs. In all these cases the objectives of leaders were supported by a reinterpretation of selected parts of the supposedly eternal and changeless Word of God.

This ability to selectively interpret the holy book is basic to the power of fundamentalist leaders. They can highlight the differences from modernism by selecting for the attention of the faithful those elements of the book which most differentiate them. So their preoccupation with developing stern doctrines relating to sexual morality is a direct contrast with promiscuous modernism. This enables leaders to create a clear distinction between the faithful and their secular enemy on an issue about which they have chosen to fight. Their choice of issue may derive from their perception of a general contemporary anxiety about the fate of the family. By their choice of particular texts, and by their new interpretation of those texts, leaders mandate themselves to do what they want to do.

Moreover, selective interpretation allows leaders to most effectively meet the needs of their followers. The Protestant fundamentalist emphasis on the doctrines of the atonement and the last days helps their followers feel uniquely safe and privileged, and leads them to believe that they have a unique insight into the future of the world. The concentration on martyrdom by the leaders of Hamas provides the hope of glory for young people about to kill others and themselves simultaneously. It is those leaders who are ideologues rather than organisers who can change belief systems in this way.[40]

Armed with control over the BVNs which motivate behaviour, fundamentalist leaders are in a favourable position to exercise considerable influence over their followers. They also have several other advantages which cement their power. They invariably claim that they have been called by God to take up leadership positions.[41] They present themselves as exemplifying the qualities of an ideal member of the group. Protestant leaders tell stories of their own redemption from sin, call to their ministry, temptation by the Devil and victory over that temptation, even though they sometimes have some difficulty in finding sufficiently heinous sins of which to repent. Muslim and Jewish leaders claim to inherit the mantle of great leaders of their religious tradition of the past. Khomeini, for example, claimed to be the supreme expert in Islamic law, directly descended from the original imams.

Once followers have internalised the movement's BVNs, leaders have little need to maintain doctrinal purity or control errant behaviour. Their followers control themselves. Rather, the only internal challenges are likely to come from those who are personally disaffected with the leader, and splits in the movement may result. The other major threat to the leader's position is his own vulnerability to the temptations of modernism. One of the reasons why the moral majority lost its impetus towards the end of the 1980s was that several of its leaders succumbed to sexual or financial scandal. However, in general, leaders of fundamentalist movements have been able to create the change they want, either by their ideological impact on BVNs, or by their organisational and political skills. So, for example, Rev. Jerry Falwell persuaded the dry and doctrinal fundamentalists and the emotional charismatic Pentecostals to join forces in the moral majority.[42]

Another achievement of fundamentalist leaders has been to set the agenda by choosing the issues on which to fight. They have rapidly responded to what they perceive as dangerous secular trends, for example the general acceptance of gays by the media.

Or, they have noted some of the weak points in the secular armour and probed them. Realising the public's disillusionment with much of modern science, they reassert the supernatural. Noting parents' fears about education, they press for school prayers and the teaching of sexual abstinence. Seeing the large number of unemployed graduates, they set about recruiting intelligent revolutionaries.

While these moves are tactical in nature, fundamentalist leaders have also been successfully strategic. They have noted major changes afoot in the world, and have anticipated or adapted to them. American Protestant leaders have recognised the increasing importance of individual spiritual exploration and development of the self for the average American. They have consequently offered a wide range of consumer experiences to suit demographic groups and meet a variety of personal needs. Fundamentalist Muslim leaders have noted the new imperialist ambitions of the neo-conservative ideologues behind President George W. Bush, and have concentrated their followers' hostility on America the Great Satan.

More generally, leaders have acted strategically in terms of their mode of operation. There have been times when they have withdrawn their forces from the fray in order to regroup. This happened in America after the Scopes trial in the 1920s, and also after the sex and financial scandals of the 1980s. In Egypt, the persecution of fundamentalist Muslims has led many to go underground and prepare for revolution. There have also been times when leaders have persuaded their followers to engage peacefully in the political process. The 1980s in America and the 1990s in Israel are examples. Finally, leaders have moved into attack mode, especially when their secular enemies have provided them with a justification for so doing. Reconstructionist Protestants wishing to conquer the world for God and engineer a theocratic majority have flourished in America especially since 9/11. Militant Jews have fought more vigorously for the land of Eretz Israel since the Palestinians proclaimed the intifada. Some Muslim leaders in Iraq have responded violently to the American and British invasion of 2003.

So the *authority* of the sacred book, and the *selection* of key elements within it, are distinctive features of fundamentalisms which serve to enhance leaders' power over their followers. Because leaders can rely on their followers' enthusiastic embrace of the movement's BVNs, they can concentrate on mobilising their support in order to achieve their strategic objectives. Indeed, such support is typically motivated by the changes in traditional religious BVNs which the fundamentalist leaders have brought about.

However, the fifth and final distinctive feature of fundamentalisms, *millennialism*, also adds to the power of fundamentalist BVNs to motivate action. Millennialism refers to a belief in the ultimate future victory of God over evil. Order will be restored to a chaotic and fallen world. Such belief is particularly prominent in American Protestantism, but is also to be found in some Muslim doctrines, where there is an expectation of the return of the Hidden Imam. Moreover, for Gush Emunim the Jewish settlement of Eretz Israel is a necessary condition for the subsequent redemption of the world. The prospect of God's ultimate triumph gives adherents the confidence that they are contributing to victory, even though it may not happen within their lifetime, and even though they do not seem to be winning at present. This long-term confidence seems more typical of militant Muslims than of others. Indeed, one of the preoccupations of some American Protestant leaders is to persuade adherents that the last days are fast approaching. Christ will return in our lifetime, and the faithful will be raptured up to be with him in heaven, while the apocalyptic battle of Armageddon is fought down here on earth. Then God will establish his millennium, or thousand years of divine rule on earth, and the faithful will return to exercise authority on his behalf.[43]

The prospect of a final struggle and a victorious outcome against a deadly foe clearly strengthens adherents' belief that their experience is to be interpreted in terms of a struggle to the death against evil. Their reactive and dualistic beliefs are strengthened by the millennialist story. More specifically, several fundamentalisms maintain that it is possible for believers to secure or hasten the millennial victory. Moreover, in their battle to hasten the millennium, the normal rules no longer apply. After all, this world's rules are about to be overtaken by God's.

Thus the four secondary defining features of fundamentalism – dualism, authority, selectivity and millennialism – all work together to buttress its central feature, namely, reactivity against modernism. A dualistic frame of reference makes it easier to stereotype one's opponents and dehumanise them, while strengthening one's own group. Such a clear distinction between godly 'us' and sinful 'them' makes it possible for leaders to use their authority to mobilise aggressive action against 'them'. Selectivity involves the reinterpretation of the holy text by leaders with the purpose of changing adherents' BVNs so as to motivate such action. And the cosmic and apocalyptic nature of the struggle and of God's ultimate victory gives an inspirational grandeur to the whole enterprise.

In this chapter I have sought to define and describe fundamentalism in sociological and general terms, using few and brief examples. In the next chapter I will review social identity theory, presenting it as a suitable theoretical framework for arriving at a deeper psychological understanding of the phenomenon of fundamentalism.

Chapter 2

Social identity theory

A *social* psychological theory

We are satisfied from the sociological evidence presented in the previous chapter that fundamentalism is a unique social phenomenon, and we understand to a degree why fundamentalisms have grown over the last century. However, little attention has hitherto been directed at how fundamentalisms have their impact upon individual adherents. Why do ordinary people surrender themselves to such movements, and how do the unique set of BVNs peculiar to each movement come to dominate their thinking and action?

This is essentially a psychological question. However, this does not imply that it is simply a question of *individual* psychology. It will not be successfully answered by concentrating solely on how the individual mind works. Reviews of the psychology of religion[1,2] reveal that most of the extant theory and research is concerned with such issues as the individual psychological needs which religion meets; differences in personal religious orientation and their consequences; the nature of individuals' spiritual experiences and their relationship with brain function; and the development with age of religious belief and experience. Such approaches are of limited relevance to understanding the specific phenomenon of fundamentalism, for they fail to relate the individual to the social. Furthermore, efforts to associate various individual personality traits with fundamentalist membership have by and large proved unsuccessful.[3] The issue here is rather one of *social* psychology. It is about the relationship of social movements, and the groups which constitute them, to individuals' selves and identities. Social psychology is uniquely the academic discipline which relates the social context to the individual psyche.

There are several theoretical approaches from within social psychology which offer promising avenues towards understanding fundamentalisms. For example, we could consider fundamentalisms as groups which are stigmatised for their cultural deviance, and explore their actions and beliefs as reactions to social stigma. We could examine fundamentalist movements as a form of social conflict, and refer to conflict theory. We could look at fundamentalist BVNs from the perspectives of social representation theory or attribution theory. And we could treat fundamentalisms as linguistic communities, sharing a common and distinctive language and based on a unique and authoritative text.

If I were to attempt to apply all the available theory and evidence from social psychology to the understanding of fundamentalisms, this would be a very long book. Doubtless, many additional theoretical insights might be obtained from such an eclectic review. However, my purpose is not only to apply social psychology to the issue in question in order to enhance our understanding of it. It is also to demonstrate that a single broad theoretical perspective can by itself provide an overall understanding and point to practical solutions. I want to show that there is still mileage in a grand theoretical narrative.

There appears to be no other theoretical perspective which offers as inclusive and powerful an explanation for the whole range of fundamentalist phenomena as does social identity theory (SID).

Throughout this book I will, for the sake of simplicity, unite two distinct historical theoretical strands under the label SID.[4,5,6,7] These are, first, the original social identity theory, inspired by Henri Tajfel, and second, self-categorisation theory, developed most notably by John Turner. The former examined how group membership leads to the formation of social identities which enhance self-esteem; the latter concentrated upon the ways in which social identities operate as social categories within the self-concept. Recently, scholars such as Michael Hogg have treated both historical strands within the same overall conceptual framework.

SID is a wide-ranging theoretical perspective, which encompasses both group relations and individual identities within its purview. More important, it gives a clear account of the relationship between the group and the individual levels of analysis. This makes it an ideal candidate for explaining fundamentalisms as social movements, but at the same time elucidating the nature of their effect upon individual adherents. When giving examples in the rest of this chapter to illustrate the theory's main ideas, I will take them from fundamentalisms. However, these merely serve for the purpose of illustration; specific propositions regarding fundamentalisms derived from SID are to be found in Chapter 3.

The theory is supported by a huge amount of evidence, derived both from the psychological laboratory and from real-life settings. However, for the sake of brevity and readability, the references in this chapter will largely be to secondary sources, where primary references to research evidence may be found. While SID itself is well supported, its application to the phenomenon of fundamentalism certainly is not. Chapter 3, however, will review evidence about fundamentalism which at least is not incompatible with the theory.

Social identity and the self

SID asserts that 'people define and evaluate themselves in terms of groups to which they belong'.[8] That is, they see themselves, at least in part, as having a social identity. I am a pious and faithful Muslim, and God has chosen me to do His will. I am a Bible-believing Baptist, and God has reserved a place in heaven for me. I am a Haredi Jew, and God honours those like me who scrupulously obey the Torah.

Social identities are to be distinguished from personal identities. The former are derived from group memberships, and regulate group behaviour. The latter are derived from the individual's unique blend of experience and characteristics, and direct individual and interpersonal behaviour. An individual's actions may be predominantly directed by either of these two types of identity. Which will predominate is predicted by several different factors. For example, if the current world situation is perceived as a struggle to the death between two sides, then social identification with one's own side will predominate. If one lives in a highly individualistic country, such as America,[9,10] then, other things being equal, personal identity will predominate. Of course, other things are not at present equal, since President Bush has persuaded large numbers of his compatriots that they are indeed engaged as a nation in a war against evil. In most Arab countries, on the other hand, the more collectivist culture will naturally lead to a predominance of social identities. Hence social identities are already primed to be activated in the present geopolitical context.

Social and personal identities are thus very important, in so far as they direct people's behaviour. Social identities direct that behaviour which relates to groups. That is, they regulate and motivate the sorts of behaviour in which members of groups engage as members. Such behaviour may include conformity with the group and cohesion within it; the stereotyping of members of other groups; favouritism towards members of one's own group; and discrimination against members of other groups. For example, the typical fundamentalist movement requires a high level of conformity among its members to its BVNs, and it benefits from the cohesion that results. It treats members of the mainstream religion from which it is derived as faithless apostates. Its members regard themselves as uniquely blessed, and treat others as inferior.

None of these theoretical proposals may seem very surprising. After all, we are fully aware that different interest groups exist, and seek to further their own interests, often at the expense of the interests of others. And differences in ideology and belief, leading to frequently bloody conflict between groups, are the familiar stuff of history. However, what prompted the development of SID in the 1960s were some extraordinary findings by Henri Tajfel and colleagues.[11] These suggested that none of these usual factors needed to be present for people to feel that they were members of a group (i.e. develop a social identity), and to engage in behaviour which favoured their own group at the expense of another.

The researchers allocated boys to one of two groups. They told them that they were being allocated on the basis of their (trivial) preference for one modern artist over another, or on the basis of their judgement about how many dots were being presented on a screen. In fact, the researchers were deceiving the boys; the allocation to the two groups was totally random. The boys were then each tasked with assigning points to an anonymous member of their own group, and to a member of the other group (but never to themselves). They never met any other boys in person. The points could subsequently be converted into money.

Thus there was no history of conflict or cooperation between the members of these two groups. There was no possibility of the boys being more socially attracted towards one of the recipients of the points than the other, since they never met them. There was no personal gain to be had, since the points (money) were allocated to others, not to oneself. There was, in other words, no apparent reason for a member of one group to discriminate against a member of the other. Yet discriminate they did, awarding more points to members of their own group than to members of the other. In a second similar experiment, boys were given the choice between being fair; giving the greatest possible reward to the two recipients; giving the greatest total reward to the in-group member; and maximising the difference between what the in-group member received and what the out-group member received. They reliably chose the last of these four outcomes. In other words, they were not so much concerned to maximise the gain of their fellow group member as to render them wealthier than the out-group member.

The results of this research served to emphasise the importance of social identity in determining social behaviour. For there seemed no other explanation possible than that the boys acted as they did because they believed themselves to be members of a group. But why should this belief motivate them to discriminate against the other group? And why, as subsequent research showed, should they evaluate their fellow group members, whom they had never even met, as more flexible, kind, and fair?[12]

The answer lies in the relationship between social identity and the self. The boys needed to boost their own group and downgrade the other because their feeling of membership of their own group was (temporarily) part of their selves. Therefore, by boosting their group they were boosting their selves. They were increasing their self-esteem. The greater the difference which they could bring about in favour of their own group (i.e. the greater the *positive distinctiveness* of their group), the greater the boost to their self-esteem. Thus there was every reason for them to accentuate the differences between their own and the other group as much as they could.

The research was taken to support the following propositions: people can very easily come to believe that they belong to a group (i.e. acquire a social identity); this belief can lead them to favour their own group relative to another; and such biased behaviour is motivated by the need to enhance one's self-esteem. The corollary, of course, is that if one perceives the group to be threatened, then one's self-esteem and social identity is threatened too. A threat to the self may cause fear, and this in turn may lead to aggression. Conflict is likely to ensue.

These conclusions have led to a popular belief that as soon as we believe we belong to some group or other, we have a natural propensity to engage in personal bias and thence inter-group conflict. SID certainly does not support such an inference, how-ever. Rather, the theory argues that, for personal bias and inter-group conflict to occur in the real world, various conditions have to be met.[13] Before I describe these conditions, however, it is important to clarify the nature of such psychological constructs as 'self' and 'identity', and the roles that they play in SID.

Hitherto, social identities have been referred to in terms of constituting part of the self. This implies that identities and the self are in some sense structured, solid and unchanging. However, SID does not make these assumptions. Rather, the self is seen essentially as a way of organising one's experience, which changes as a function of changes in that experience.[14] We develop selves because we are capable of being *reflexive*; we can, for example, make inferences about the sort of people we are from observing our own behaviour. Self-awareness and self-esteem are conse-quences of this capacity to be reflexive. We also base our selves on others' reactions to us; the self is an essential element of social interaction. We can, however, present our self in such a way as to affect those reactions. Further, our social self will in turn affect the nature of our perceptions of others. Because we have a social identity as a born-again believer, for example, we will perceive others in terms of their belief or lack of it. And finally, we use our selves to direct our behaviour towards others; the self has an agentive and motivating function, directing choices and seeking to control outcomes. The directive function of the self is also exercised in self-control; the self has to monitor itself while also directing behaviour.

Two things are clear from this very brief review of the concept of the self. First, it is very central to the psychology of the person and second, it is largely social in nature, both in terms of its derivation from social experience, and also in terms of its regulation of social behaviour. The self is in a constant dynamic relationship with the person's social environment, both acting upon that environment and being acted upon by it.

Likewise, social identities, as part of the self, are not fixed and static in nature. Rather, the belief that one is a member of the moral majority, for example, may change in nature as one meets more of one's fellow majority members in the course of cam-paigning for the abolition of abortion. Also, one's set of social identities may change its composition. I may stop believing myself to be a member of the moral majority when its leaders behave immorally, and consequently reaffirm my identity as a Bible-believing Baptist.

The relationship of the self to social identities now becomes clearer. Social identities become integrated into the self. The belief that one belongs to a particular group may become internalised and part of the self. Since the self has a directive function, it follows that social identity can be used to direct behaviour. Individuals then behave as group members. Their actions are those of, for example, a radical Muslim or a born-again Christian. They are no longer those of Mohammed Atta or Howard Ahmanson as unique individuals with personal identities, but rather of those same persons as members of categories to which they perceive themselves to belong.[15] Please note that these categories do not necessarily represent actual physical groups of people. The categories of 'born-again believers' and 'the secular world', for example, are more abstract, and represent categories within the mind of the Protestant fundamentalist.

The context for social identities

We may now return to the conditions which have to be operative before our social identities can lead us into biased and conflictual behaviour. The first condition is obvious. A social identity first has to be in a position to direct our behaviour if it is to lead us into conflict. Now, we are each likely to possess several different social identities. We believe ourselves, in other words, to belong to several social groups or categories. We may therefore ask: what determines which particular social identity from among the several that we possess will direct our behaviour in any given situation?

The first condition for a social identity to direct our behaviour is that it should be strongly internalised into the self. However, we may well ask how strong is strongly? The results of Tajfel's classic experiments suggest that it does not take much to ensure that a social identity directs group behaviour. We should remember, however, that the experimental situation was such that there were no other clues given as to how one should behave apart from the allocation into groups. Most social situations are far more complex than this, and a wide range of alternative social responses are possible. From among the variety of social identities available to direct these responses, it is probable that, other things being equal, a social identity which is centrally important to the self, and which frequently directs the person's behaviour, will be dominant and accessible. So, for example, a male Haredi Jew will find himself in many social situations where a variety of Jews are present. Because of the centrality of his Haredi social identity to his self and his frequent use of it, he is likely to direct his behaviour towards his fellow Jews on the basis of that identity, rather than on the basis of a Jewish social identity, an Israeli one, or even an identity as a human being. As a consequence, he may well treat them as an out-group.

The second condition for a social identity to direct behaviour relates to the immediate social context of that behaviour. The context has to provide opportunity for comparison and competition between groups. In other words, individuals have to perceive other groups to be present in the social context. Of course, these perceptions are likely to be individuals' constructions of the situation; and in their turn, such constructions are likely to derive from their own group memberships and beliefs. For example, born-again Christians may construe a social situation such as a party or a workplace as one in which most of the others present are unsaved sinners. In this case, the centrality of their born-again social identity to their selves has rendered it already relatively salient in their minds. It has also directed their perception of the situation to construe two groups present, the saved and the unsaved. And, in a circular social dynamic, their perception of the presence of unsaved persons reinforces their own saved social identity. However, if the social situation were a meeting of members of their local church, they would be unlikely to construe it in terms of saved versus unsaved groups. Rather, they might, for example, construe it as those experienced in the faith versus those recently converted to it; or as male church members as opposed to female ones, given that different norms of behaviour are required of each gender.[16,17]

This example highlights the importance of the situational context in determining which social identity is salient (or uppermost in our minds) and directs behaviour. A major feature of that context is, of course, the nature and relevance of the perceived out-group (the unsaved) to the salient social identity. In this case the symbiosis is only too clear. In categorising the others as unsaved, the fundamentalist believers are necessarily emphasising that they themselves are saved.

What else determines which other categories or groups are perceived in a social situation, and hence which of one's own identities becomes salient and directs behaviour? A very important feature of SID is the so-called *meta-contrast principle*.[18] This states that the salience of a social identity is accentuated when the differences within one's own category are less than the differences between one's own and another category. Hence a social identity will be particularly salient if the similarities within one's own category, and the differences with an out-group, are both maximised. We have to be as like each other as possible, and as different as possible from 'them'. Thus *self-categorisation is a context-determined process based on sensitivity to relative differences*.[19]

So, for example, faced with an evolutionary scientist arguing for a non-creationist curriculum on the school board of which he was also a member, a Southern Baptist would likely join forces with the other born-again believers on the board. His born-again identity would be salient because he perceives himself to hold the same BVNs as his co-believers, and to hold markedly different ones from the scientist and her supporters. On the other hand, suppose the context is an evangelical conference, convened to listen to a prominent preacher expounding the Bible. There may be people from three different local suburban mega-churches present. However, these social identities as church members are unlikely to become salient because, while each of these groups may be fairly homogeneous within itself, the difference with the other churches is not perceived to be great, particularly in the context of a shared event with a common purpose.

There are, moreover, certain cognitive processes which help to maximise similarities within, and differences between, social categories. These processes can be jointly termed *depersonalisation*.[20] This refers to the tendency to pay attention to those characteristics of the person which represent his or her social identity, and to ignore those which represent his or her personal identity. In other words, the BVNs and other characteristics of the group are attributed to all its members, with the result that differences between them are minimised. Members are, as it were, interchangeable. This applies to one's own group, where the resulting set of commonly held characteristics is known as a *prototype*. It also applies to the out-group, where it is termed a *stereotype*. These processes obviously serve to minimise the differences within groups. They also increase the probability that the groups will be seen as different from each other. For if there were a wide range of differences within each group, overlap between the groups by means of their outlying members would be more likely. The groups would not be totally distinct from each other. Social comparisons and consequent social distinctions between them would be less likely and so, therefore, would conflict.

For example, fundamentalist believers of all religions have clearly defined BVNs, legitimised by the holy book, or by their leadership, or by both. These enable them to sharply distinguish themselves from secular groups. They also tend to stereotype secular people as having a particular common set of godless BVNs, ignoring the manifold differences in the secular world. Hence fundamentalists achieve maximum similarity within the group and maximum differentiation from 'the world' by means of their own prototype and their stereotype of the other. Conflict becomes more probable.

Let us consider the implications of prototyping. The sharing of BVNs and other characteristics within the group has several important implications. First, it emphasises the importance of conformity. In order to establish and maintain conformity, those who wish to become adherents have to embrace the new (to them) BVNs. Given that these are usually counter-cultural, various means of ensuring conformity have to be employed. These may include the use by the convert of the strange new language code in which the BVNs are expressed.[21,22] They may also have to change their appearance in order to signal that they have given up sinful, especially sexually sinful, values.[23]

Prototypes are fuzzy sets of characteristics which are believed to describe group members. Some features are particularly powerful in distinguishing the group from others. For example, such norms of behaviour as dress, beard and hair may serve such a purpose for fundamentalist Jews and Sikhs. Or certain features of the belief system may single out adherents from others, such as the belief of many American Protestants in the importance of a single moment of conversion to the faith, when the sinner is forgiven once and for all.[24] Some members will demonstrate these differentiating features to a greater degree than others, and hence will be more prototypical. Leaders are likely to emerge from those who are extremely prototypical, thereby being respected for being a model member. This may later gain them 'idiosyncracy credit'; in other words, having earned their leadership role the hard way, they have permission from their followers to become less prototypical and more innovative.[25]

Being prototypical, then, is one of the means by which in-groups can distinguish themselves from out-groups. However, like other elements of the self, prototypes are not static. Rather they change as the social context changes. For example, when the comparison is with the apostate church, fundamentalists tend to place doctrinal correctness in the forefront of their prototype. When, however, the comparison is with certain 'immoral' secular groups, value positions on the relevant social issues become more important features. When the out-group is the evil secular world in general, the prototype is dominated by the fervour with which the dualistic ideological worldview and the metaphor of warfare are embraced. Conflict now appears inevitable.

Moreover, the more general and inclusive the out-group becomes, the more extreme the in-group's prototype.[26] This is because the out-group is now so obviously varied that only an extreme prototype will differentiate the in-group from all out-group members. As a consequence of this extremity of the prototype, the group's leadership is likely to be more extreme; and such a leadership will seek to define the out-group with even greater generality. For example, the scholarly Muslim clerics arguing against less conservative believers give way to militant ideologues seeking to overthrow nominally Muslim governments or even America, the Great Satan.

Stereotypes serve a similar function, permitting the in-group to see itself as more distinct from a uniform out-group. An interesting feature of stereotypes is that they tend to attribute the set of unfavourable out-group features as entirely due to the characters of the out-group members.[27] The notion that the situation in which the out-group finds itself might be a reason for its BVNs is not entertained. This 'dispositional', as opposed to 'situational', attribution enables the out-group to be scapegoated. For example, 'Muslims act as they do because they are the sort of people that they are: medieval fanatics'.

Thus, in summary, social context is crucial, both in determining whether *any* social identity becomes salient and so directs behaviour; and also in determining *which* social identity becomes salient in a particular situation, and whether conflict ensues. The third condition for a social identity to become salient is that *the out-group has to be relevant*. SID has emphasised that the identity and nature of the out-group will decide the nature of the in-group prototype. But what determines the choice of out-group in the first place? SID proposes that there are two such determinants: the degree of *security* that the in-group feels, and the degree of *permeability* of the in-group and out-group.[28]

Where there is a threat to the in-group's social identity, this will cause insecurity. The threat can be to the very survival of the category itself: for example, 'the existence of our faith is threatened by the secular world'. It can be to the category's distinctiveness: 'our standards of holy behaviour are becoming lax'. It may be to its value: 'little respect is shown to us and our status is lowered'. And it may be to its acceptance: 'people refuse us our right to worship and evangelise freely'.[29] Whatever the nature of the threat to social identity, insecurity will increase.

If the boundaries around the groups are impermeable, then it will be in vain to try to leave the in-group, perhaps to join the out-group. Very few new ideas will enter the group's consciousness. The boundaries round the in-group may be self-imposed, in an effort to maintain the prototype and distinguish the group from others. A combination of impermeability and insecurity is therefore highly likely to result in the selection of an out-group to scapegoat, and in consequent conflict. The in-group has nothing to lose; its members are stuck where they are, and they feel threatened. All they can do is fight.

Group perceptions

It is clear that comparison of one's own group or category with others is a major cause of conflict. Recent research has emphasised the importance of the in-group's perceptions of itself in relation to out-groups. In particular, in-groups are frequently concerned about their relative status, and also the extent to which they are in a minority position numerically. They are, of course, concerned because these factors have an effect upon their selves. If my group is of low status, then my self is of lower value, since my group identity is part of my self. It is important to note that these two factors, *relative status* and *minority position*, are unrelated, and have separate and different effects.[30]

The subjective nature of these perceptions on the part of in-group members permits them to construe their relative status differently from the way it is construed by others. So, for example, a fundamentalist movement may be regarded by much of the rest of society as consisting of uneducated people lacking in social status. However, the movement's members may see themselves as

God's agents, empowered to rule the rebellious world on His behalf, and of high status in His eyes. It is their own perception of their status, rather than the perceptions of others, which affects their social identities. They often engage in such social creativity to transform their status.[31]

Perceptions of relative status have profound effects on social identities. Those who believe their group to be of high status perceive it to be more homogeneous, and identify more strongly with it.[32] Greater homogeneity, as we have seen, makes it more likely that members will consider themselves to be different from other groups. And stronger identification results in greater commitment to the group and its aims.[33]

The same is true of the perception that one is in a minority. Such a perception only results in a stronger identification with the group. And when this minority perceives itself to be threatened, its strong social identity results in increased solidarity and mutual association.[34] The tendency of fundamentalists to perceive themselves as a minority under threat of destruction by secular society is thus in reality an effective survival mechanism.

How does an enhanced social identity increase commitment to the group? It is argued that there are three components to any social identity: a *cognitive* element, which is the belief that one belongs to the social category; an *evaluative* element, by which one compares the category to others; and an *affective* element, the extent to which one feels committed to it. Research demonstrates that high perceived status contributes to a high evaluation of one's group and to group commitment. Perception of being in a minority, however, only strengthens one's belief that one belongs (the cognitive component of the group identity). Moreover, if someone believes that they have chosen to join a group rather than simply been allocated to it, they are more likely to be committed. Thus, fundamentalists who believe themselves to have chosen the path of salvation and who consider themselves of high spiritual status relative to the sinful world are likely to be highly committed. And it is their commitment which leads them to act as loyal group members in the fight against their adversaries.[35]

In sum, group members' perceptions of their own group, their out-groups and the comparisons they make between them relating to status have a potent effect upon the strength and salience of their group social identity and hence their commitment to act on its behalf.

Self-esteem and meaning

We have examined the contribution made by SID to the under-standing of group behaviour, and how category membership can become part of the self. However, there remains the question of why individuals join groups, and internalise the social category, together with its associated BVNs. What psychological needs does membership satisfy? SID proposes two fundamental motivations: the need for self-esteem and the reduction of uncertainty.

The motivating power of self-esteem has already been discussed. When our group is threatened, then so is our social identity. Our social identity is part of our selves, and therefore our selves are in danger and our self-esteem threatened. A victory for our group, or an increase in its status, on the other hand, enhances our self-esteem. Fundamentalisms, for example, tend to look to enhance their self-esteem by means of victory, rather than by increasing their status in social terms. This is because of the following basic contradiction: if one achieves status in the eyes of the secular world, then by definition one must be failing to fight the good fight. Persecution by 'the world' proves that one is being faithful. As I suggested in the previous section, it is status in the eyes of God which matters. American Protestant fundamentalists have fre-quently wavered in their position about status. They gain self-esteem when the president is one of their own, and when Billy Graham visits the Oval Office. But they retreat into greater iso-lation when their attempts at political influence fail. It is far safer and easier to feel superior to a stereotyped out-group.

Status may, of course, be gained within the social category. For example, in Christian Protestant fundamentalism, one's congrega-tion or denomination may be growing faster than any other. In this case the category of congregation or denomination would be *nested* within the over-arching category of born-again believer: the basic BVNs would be the same, but the sub-category would have a few additional features. One may alternatively strive to polish up one's prototype so that one is holier than fellow adherents. Or self-esteem may be gained, not by enhanced status, but simply by the very fact of belonging. These people welcome me and accept me as one of them (provided I think, feel, speak, and act as they do). Now I am one of us.

Another major psychological need which is met by social identi-ties is the need to *reduce uncertainty*.[36] The major element of social identities are the BVNs with which they are associated. These are internalised as part of the social identity, and become part of the self. If, for example, the social identity is that of fundamentalist believer, then this is likely to be a dominant and frequently salient identity, and to be used to regulate one's actions in a great variety of situations. The clear and explicit set of fundamentalist BVNs therefore enables adherents to reduce their uncertainty about their selves. When adherents see that their fellow adherents agree with them about what are the right BVNs to hold, and when they perceive out-groups to disagree, then they can be all the more certain that they are correct. Hence they can be more certain about their selves.

Fundamentalist BVNs make it clear how we should act, what attitudes about various issues we should hold, what values we should prioritise and what we should believe. They present us with a worldview which enables us to place ourselves clearly within it. They give us a view of history in which the part we have to play is revealed to us. For example, the world is the stage for a struggle to the death between the faithful and the Great Satan. Our own reward for furthering the ultimate victory in that struggle is to achieve the status of martyr. Or, we have accepted Christ as our Saviour by virtue of his atoning sacrifice on the Cross. We will be raptured up into the heavens when he appears, and when he finally rules, we will be given positions of authority in his kingdom.[37]

Another advantage of BVNs is that they enable us to predict the actions of members of other groups and plan accordingly. This is because we hold our in-group's stereotypes of out-groups, and so we believe that we know the sort of people they are and therefore the way they are going to behave. Our stereotypes will also lead us to behave towards them in ways which make it probable that they will respond in the way we expect, the self-fulfilling prophecy.[38] This capacity to predict, and therefore plan for, the actions of others also serves to increase our self-esteem. For we can feel ourselves to have some control over what happens to us, and to be less at risk.

The need for certainty is by definition likely to be greater when uncertainty is perceived to be high. Perceptions of uncertainty will be high when there are threats to our social identities, of the types described above. For example, the perceived threat to their very existence obviously obsesses some militant fundamentalists. But the threat of dilution of the pure BVNs, and of stereotypes and prototypes, by contact with out-groups has also been a dominant theme in fundamentalist thinking. The more contact they have with the secular world, the more adherents may see that there are alternative BVNs to the very unusual ones they hold. Perhaps this is why there is a marked generational effect in fundamentalisms.[39] The first generation may have actually undergone a conversion experience and made a clean break with their former selves. Their children often have no such experience, and are more open to secular alternatives. Perhaps, they think, things aren't so certain after all.

There are many other sources of uncertainty in the modern world. In particular, the process of industrialisation has resulted in large numbers of people moving to cities, having left behind their rural communities, extended families and traditional BVNs. The new urban proletariat are therefore a rich source of recruitment for fundamentalisms. Whatever the reason for uncertainty, however, it is quite clear how fundamentalisms can reduce it. They can re-emphasise their distinctiveness from other groups, thereby creating harder prototypes and stereotypes. Prototypes reduce one's uncertainty about who one is, stereotypes about who others are and therefore how to behave towards them. Fundamentalist leaders can redefine doctrine and selectively emphasise certain beliefs so as to give meaning and purpose to their adherents in their current situation. They can reinforce certain values and attitudes, so that adherents know how to think and feel about other groups. And they can specify norms of behaviour which help the individual take those behavioural choices which face them in a secular world. In times of great uncertainty, when social identities and therefore selves are threatened, leaders are likely to be strong and proto-typical, and to encourage conflictual inter-group behaviour. For these are the ways to clarify and strengthen a social identity.[40]

Social groups with a strong social identity carry all sorts of advantages. To sum up as far as the individual is concerned:

> it is aversive to be uncertain about beliefs, attitudes, feelings and behaviours that one feels are important to one's sense of who one is. Group identification is a particularly effective way to reduce such uncertainty, because the process of deperson-alisation associated with self-categorisation transforms the 'uncertain self' into a 'certain self' governed by an in-group prototype that is consensually validated by fellow in-group

members. In this way, group membership accentuates proto-typical similarity. It also resolves uncertainty and imbues the group with positive valence that generalises to self and fellow group members, and thus generates positive group evaluations (ethnocentrism ingroup bias), positive self-evaluation (self-esteem), and positive evaluation of fellow members (social attraction).[41]

However, the advantages of uncertainty reduction via a strong social identity do not accrue only to individual group members. They also apply to the group as a whole and to its leaders. For a group which has a clear and strong social identity is likely to believe its members to be similar to each other. They are therefore likely to like and trust each other, communicate clearly, influence each other, and cooperate and act collectively. Hence successful collective action will be possible. Such groups can be mobilised for social and political action.[42]

In summary, SID provides a convincing account of why people are motivated to join social groups. It specifies the conditions under which those groups are more likely to be in conflict with others. These include the degree of identification of the members with the group; the extent to which the social context permits group members to make comparisons of their own group with others; and the relevance of the out-group to the in-group. SID suggests the reasons why a particular social identity becomes salient in the individual's mind so that it directs his or her behaviour. It also suggests the cognitive mechanisms, such as the development of prototypes and of stereotypes, by means of which members construe themselves and their social environment. Above all, SID makes clear the relationships between the features of groups and the selves of their members, using the concept of social identity as its lynchpin. As a consequence of its clarification of the relationships between group membership and the self, SID represents an extremely powerful tool for understanding fundamentalisms and their members.

Chapter 3

Psychological evidence

Hypotheses from SID

The account of SID in the previous chapter used examples from fundamentalisms in order to clarify the elements of the theory. Hopefully, these suggested that the theory's application to fundamentalism might be illuminating. However, there is no substitute for deriving specific hypotheses based on the theory, and then reviewing the existing evidence to determine the extent to which these hypotheses are supported. In this chapter I will review the literature from the psychological study of religion, but with the caveat that none of this research has been explicitly undertaken to test hypotheses derived from SID. In the following two chapters, I will present two case studies in order to add to this somewhat piecemeal evidence.

There are some specific hypotheses which may be derived from each of the main features of SID, in the light of the accounts of fundamentalism and of SID in the previous chapters. The first and most obvious are:

1 Members of a fundamentalist movement will have a more salient and central religious social identity than non-fundamentalist religious believers.
2 Their movement's prototype of itself and its stereotype(s) of its out-group(s) will be more internally homogeneous than those of non-fundamentalist religious movements.
3 Their movement's prototype will differ more from its stereotype(s) than is the case for non-fundamentalist religious movements.

The next four hypotheses derive directly or indirectly from the concepts of prototypes, stereotypes and the meta-contrast principle (see pp. 32–33). They are as follows:

4 The greater the homogeneity of the prototype held of itself by a fundamentalist movement, the more different from that prototype will be the stereotype(s) which it holds of its out-group(s).

5 The greater the homogeneity of the prototype, and the greater its difference from the stereotype(s) of its out-group(s), the more salient will be a fundamentalist movement's social identity in the minds of its adherents.

6 The greater the inclusiveness of a fundamentalist movement's out-group(s), the more extreme and homogeneous will be its own prototype.

7 The more homogeneous, extreme and salient a fundamentalist movement's prototype, the greater will be the degree of conflict in which it is engaged.

Thus, if the first three hypotheses of differences between fundamentalist and non-fundamentalist religious movements are supported, it follows from the next four that:

8 Fundamentalist movements will be more likely to engage in conflict than non-fundamentalist movements.

The next hypothesis derives from the contextual principles of SID (see pp. 34–35):

9 The greater a fundamentalist movement's insecurity and impermeability, the more homogeneous, extreme and salient its prototype, and the greater the degree of conflict in which it is engaged.

The final hypotheses derive from the motivational features of SID (see pp. 37–40):

10 Individuals' self-esteem and certainty are negatively related to the probability of their joining a fundamentalist movement, and positively related to length of membership.

11 The greater the difference between a fundamentalist movement's prototype and its stereotype(s) of its out-group(s), the
higher will be its adherents' self-esteem and certainty.
12 The more homogeneous a fundamentalist group's prototype
and its stereotype(s) of its out-group(s), the higher will be its
adherents' self-esteem and certainty.

Again it follows, if hypotheses 1–3 are supported, that:

13 The self-esteem and certainty of the adherents of fundamentalist movements will be higher than that of the adherents of
non-fundamentalist religious movements.

Obviously, it is a major task to operationalise the constructs of
SID sufficiently reliably and validly for these hypotheses to be
tested, either in field or in laboratory studies. For example, how
might one estimate how extreme a prototype is, or measure degree
of conflict? However, there are good measures available for some of
the constructs (e.g. self-esteem and prejudicial attitudes). In the
following review of the literature, I will select four areas of research
which relate to the hypotheses. They are, first, about *sects and their
popularity* despite their strictness; second regarding *prejudice against
out-groups*; third, concerning *religious attributions* of the causality of
events; and finally, about *cognitive complexity and rigidity*. Usually,
however, because of the different constructs and measures used, any
support which the literature provides for SID will be indirect and
inferential in nature.

There are additional reasons why it is difficult to support SID
from the existing literature. The empirical psychological research
on religion has been conducted almost entirely in America. The
consequences are several. First, the samples are overwhelmingly of
Christians, and usually Protestant ones at that, and a high proportion of the respondents are students. And more important, the
initial orientation from which most scholars approach the issues is
one of individual differences, both as predictor and as outcome
variables. Thus such variables as beliefs (especially attributions of
causality), values and attitudes, together with more specific variables, such as orientation towards religion and right-wing authoritarianism, are frequent predictors in the research literature.

Within this individualistic framework, fundamentalism is meas-
ured as degree of agreement with various statements of attitude

and belief rather than as a self-chosen categorical description of a social identity.[1,2] Hence, theoretical explanations for why fundamentalists display their various BVNs are rare. Rather, a set of empirical relationships between strength of fundamentalist beliefs and various attitudinal and behavioural constructs has been established, with varying degrees of confidence. Theoretical constructs explaining the relationship between social movements and individuals' BVNs are not readily apparent in the field, nor are motivational explanations for actions undertaken as a member of a group. A social psychological approach is normally understood in this literature to mean the study of individual differences such as attitudes and values which have a social origin. As a result, truly social psychological theories, which relate social group membership to individual psychological processes, are largely absent from the literature.

It might be argued that such measures of fundamentalism as that of Altemeyer and Hunsberger[3] are an adequate proxy for fundamentalist identities. This instrument asks respondents whether their own religious belief uniquely represents the fundamental truth; whether this truth is opposed by evil; whether the religious practices of the past have to be followed; and whether only they have a right relationship with God. While such items do sample some of the definitive features of fundamentalisms, for example, their dualism and exclusivity, the instrument seems to omit or underplay others. In particular, the central and most definitive feature of fundamentalism, its reactive hostility towards modernism, is not emphasised. Thus we do not really know the extent to which those who score high on religious fundamentalism scales have a fundamentalist social identity.

In-groups and out-groups

There is, however, one investigation which goes some way towards demonstrating such a relationship.[4] It showed that both those who scored high on the fundamentalism scale, and also those who scored high on a scale of orthodoxy of Christian belief, were more likely to have a positive attitude towards Christians and people who believe in God ($r = .46$ and $.51$ respectively). Orthodoxy was assessed in terms of assent to various central Christian beliefs, for example, the resurrection of Christ and his future return. Since one of the definitive features of fundamentalisms is their belief in the inerrancy of their doctrine and their holy book, it is likely that both the fundamentalism scale and the orthodoxy scale were assessing aspects of Christian fundamentalism. The researchers also found that high scorers held negative attitudes towards atheists and non-believers, thus demonstrating the prejudice against opposing out-groups typical of those with a strong social identity. Non-believers, moreover, were less hostile towards believers than were the believers towards them. This would be consistent with the attach-ment of a greater importance to their religious identity by funda-mentalists than by non-believers (to their secular identity). This research has awakened a long overdue interest in the idea of fundamentalisms as in-groups with prejudicial attitudes towards out-groups.

A more sociologically oriented body of research and theory on the distinction between churches and sects also supports the basic in-group versus out-group dichotomy which is the initial starting point for SID. Religious movements are to be considered as existing in a constant dynamic process of change, in which long-established movements spawn sects, which consist of those dis-satisfied with their lack of rigour and vigour. However, gradually these sects in their turn become established bureaucratic organisa-tions, and so the process continues.[5] While established churches tend to be inclusive in their membership, sects are more exclusive, requiring strict doctrinal and behavioural conformity from their members.[6] In the terminology of SID, sects are likely to have more homogeneous prototypes of the ideal or typical member than are established religious movements. The latter, being more inclusive, are less opposed to the social environment within which they exist.

If we characterise fundamentalist religious movements as sects, then it becomes clear at the historical level of analysis why they treat the mainstream versions of their religion as an immediate out-group, and the secular world as a broader one. However, an explanation in terms of SID is also apparent. The strictness of their beliefs and norms of behaviour not only results in a conformist homogeneity of their prototype, but also in opposed stereotypes of mainstream religious movements and of the secular world. Accord-ing to SID, these conditions are likely to result in the satisfaction of the motivational needs for self-esteem and meaning derived from a distinctive, exclusive and homogeneous social identity. Hence, those for whom these needs are not met by their other social identities (including their mainstream religious affiliation, if they have one) should be potential recruits for fundamentalisms. Fundamentalisms' exclusivity of membership and clarity and simplicity of doctrine satisfy their members' needs.

Indeed, SID leads to different hypotheses from the dominant theoretical model of mainstream religious movements versus sects.[7] This model suggests that in the market-place for religion, sects will attract adherents to the extent that they moderate their doctrines and practices so as to be in greater accord with the host secular culture. Thus sects will grow if they *decrease* the tension with that culture. More liberal mainstream churches, on the other hand, may have to *increase* this tension in order to be sufficiently distinctive from their secular environment to attract those seeking a religious affiliation. The psychological assumption here is one of the need for consistency within the self. Hence, social identities derived from the secular world and religious identities should not be sufficiently mutually contradictory as to cause discomfort. By way of contrast, SID predicts that members will be more attracted to fundamentalisms when their religious identity is very clearly distinguished from other social identities, whereas the 'religious market-place' theory suggests that there should be a greater degree of attraction when the fundamentalist prototype is moderated to accord more with secular social identities.

The empirical evidence[8] demonstrates that members of American Christian sects certainly hold different doctrinal beliefs and endorse different behaviours from mainstream Protestants. They are highly likely to disapprove of gambling and dancing and favour censorship; to reject Darwin; and to believe in a Devil and in Jesus' return to earth. The researchers assume that these doctrinal beliefs and behavioural attitudes are counter-cultural and will provoke mainstream hostility. However, the idea that there exists a single liberal dominant culture in America is open to question, at the very least. When we learn, for example, that according to a CNN poll some 59 per cent of the American population believe that the prophecies in the biblical book of Revelation will come true,[9] it is evident that fundamentalist sects are not necessarily in a cultural minority. It could be argued, on the contrary, that they constitute a continuation of a long historical strand of small town political and religious conservatism which is deeply embedded in American culture. The idea that sects are in some sense counter-cultural and in tension with a monolithic mainstream may therefore be rejected in favour of their location as a major element within a diverse and pluralist cultural patchwork. They provide an important social identity for large numbers of Americans, an identity which meets their needs for self-esteem and meaning.

In fact, patterns of church membership demonstrate clearly that a growth in fundamentalist religious affiliation has occurred relative to the declining membership of liberal 'mainstream' churches. The latter have lost members, while such denominations as the conservative Southern Baptists and the charismatic Pentecostals have gained them.[10] The literature has characterised the growth churches as being stricter and more serious,[11] or, more recently,[12] as incurring costs for their members over and above those normally associated with church membership. Laurence Iannaccone argues that stricter rules and greater demands on members require greater commitment to the church, since no 'free riding' is possible. Empirical research[13] demonstrates that such 'strictness' is indeed related to commitment expressed in time and money, and that more conservative churches, for example Southern Baptists, are more strict.

So why do stricter churches attract and retain adherents? It could be argued that they have more resources to play with because of their members' greater commitment. Maybe adherents believe that the spiritual rewards outweigh even the considerable costs involved. Or perhaps it is simply due to the demographic fact that conservative Christians have more children than others.[14] Or maybe, more generally, the stronger an individual's familial or social relationships with existing fundamentalist adherents, the more likely they are to join, despite increasing social and geographical mobility.[15,16]

However, this success of stricter churches is at the least not inconsistent with predictions based on SID. Of course, the above demographic explanations for this success are not necessarily incompatible with explanations at the psychological level of analysis. Parents or spouses, for example, might have persuaded their children or partners of the benefits of a fundamentalist social identity. The greater commitment demonstrated by fundamentalists may indicate a religious social identity which is so central and important to adherents' selves that potential secular identities can be ignored, or turned into out-groups. Strict religion requires extensive socialisation into a conformist, tightly-knit and mutually reaffirming group, which reinforces its social identity.[17] The homogeneous prototype that results enables adherents to hold stereotypes of outsiders as sinners and not to be trusted.[18] In contrast, to explain the relative growth and increased commitment of stricter churches, the 'market-place' theory would need to show that they had somehow succeeded in adapting to secular norms while remaining strict. There appears to be little such evidence.

Thus the literature on sects and adherents' commitment to them is not inconsistent with hypotheses 1 to 5 and 11 to 13 (above).

Prejudice against out-groups

If fundamentalist groups demonstrate a higher degree of prejudice against out-groups than do other religious groups, such results would be consistent with SID. For we would expect the homogeneous and extreme prototypes characteristic of fundamentalists to give rise to opposing homogeneous and extreme stereotypes of out-groups. Stereotypes may be characterised as the cognitive component of prejudiced attitudes;[19] they are beliefs about a class of people of whom we disapprove or, sometimes, approve (prejudice does not have to be negative). Moreover, we would expect negative prejudice to be directed towards those categories of person specified as out-groups by the fundamentalist movement of which the individual is an adherent. In other words, as part of the prototype of the ideal or typical member, prejudicial attitudes towards certain out-groups are among the BVNs which are attached to the movement's social identity.

In the case of American fundamentalist Protestantism, on which most of the research has been conducted, the element of biblical authority and inerrancy is of the utmost importance in their belief system. God is believed to be speaking directly to the believer through His Word, and the believer is expected to take 'what God says' at face value. Hence if it is indicated in the Bible that certain actions are forbidden, then the category of persons who engage in or support these practices are likely to be treated as a hostile out-group, and be the victims of fundamentalist prejudice. Thus SID would predict that only certain categories will be victims of prejudice: those condemned by the leadership of the fundamentalist movement, on the basis of biblical authority.

The dominant individual difference paradigm in research on the psychology of religion leads to different hypotheses, however. If fundamentalism is an individual orientation towards religion, then it will relate to other individual characteristics or styles, for example, to right-wing authoritarianism[20] or to Rokeach's construct of closed-mindedness.[21] These styles would lead to the prediction of prejudice in general, not to that of specific prejudices in particular.

The available research appears to support the predictions from SID. Research has recently been dominated by attempts to disentangle the effect on prejudicial attitudes of religious fundamentalism as a personal religious orientation from that of right-wing authoritarianism. The latter construct is defined as authoritarian submission, authoritarian aggression and conventionalism,[22,23] and derives ultimately from classic work on the authoritarian personality.[24] Results[25,26] indicate that fundamentalism is highly correlated with authoritarianism and with prejudice against gays. However, multiple regression analysis indicates that it is authoritarianism rather than fundamentalism which accounts for more of the variance in prejudice. Nevertheless, some anti-gay prejudice remains, even when authoritarianism and degree of orthodoxy are controlled for.[27] On the other hand, there is no relationship between fundamentalism and ethnic prejudice, and indeed fundamentalism is negatively correlated with ethnic prejudice when the effect of authoritarianism is controlled. In contrast, atheists and unbelievers are victims of strong fundamentalist prejudice.[28] It should be noted, however, that one relatively recent investigation found discriminatory attitudes against blacks, women, gays and communists among fundamentalists.[29]

The overall conclusion from this research is that fundamentalist American Christians are prejudiced against some categories of person but not against others. This argues against an association of fundamentalism with prejudice in general. But what does the evidence suggest regarding the origins of this differential prejudice? Batson[30] has suggested that some prejudices are actually proscribed by religious groups, whereas others are not mentioned, or are even encouraged. Fundamentalist Christians have been mobilised to fight 'the gay lobby' ever since the days of the moral majority in the 1980s, and the issue has more recently been used by fundamentalists to create schism in the Anglican Communion.[31] Similarly, American fundamentalists have recently emphasised the distinction between 'the biblical worldview' (their own) and 'the secular worldview' (everyone else's).[32] Such dualism inevitably leads to prejudice against the out-group of unbelievers, and explains the empirical finding of prejudice against them.

It is important to note that fundamentalist prejudices are against out-group members, rather than against merely the 'sin' of which they are 'guilty'. In other words, the issue is one of inter-group relationships rather than merely of doctrinal orthodoxy. Fundamentalist anti-gay prejudice is, for example, directed at gay people even though they are celibate (and not therefore committing the 'sin' of homosexuality).[33] Fundamentalist prejudice, like other prejudice, is against categories of person, and therefore against individuals *because they represent a particular category*. Their individuality is obscured by their social identity as members of an out-group; they are depersonalised.

The research on the prejudices of religious people is voluminous.[34,35] However, we may conclude that that part of it which relates to fundamentalists tends to support a theoretical approach based on inter-group relations and social identities rather than one which treats fundamentalism as an individual's religious orientation. The research taken together appears to be consistent with hypotheses 4 and 5 (above). There is also a body of research which relates to the motivations for fundamentalist affiliation, and to this we now turn.

Attributions and motivations

SID proposes that there are two major motivations for maintaining a social identity: the enhancement of self-esteem and the reduction of uncertainty. In Chapter 2 I reviewed the various ways in which these motives may operate within the SID theoretical framework of inter-group relations and social identities (see pp. 37–40). One way is through the BVNs which are part of the prototype of the social identity in question, in this case, that of a fundamentalist movement. From within this set of BVNs, needs for self-esteem and meaning may be met in several ways. For example, the belief that one has been chosen by God to act as His agent on earth is likely to enhance one's self-esteem. So is the continuous dualistic comparison of one's own sanctified identity with the stereotype of the sinful secular world. The two key Protestant fundamentalist narratives, of personal redemption and of God's control of history past, present and future, provide a comprehensive system of meaning to explain the ambiguous and uncertain world and one's own place within it.[36,37]

However, psychologically-oriented researchers into religion have concentrated much of their effort on a very specific aspect of meaning: the attribution of causality. Attributions have the obvious function of providing an explanation for an event or action which may seem unusual, or hard to understand or control.[38] They reduce uncertainty. However, they may also serve to boost self-esteem by, for example, crediting good actions or outcomes to oneself and bad ones to a variety of other causes. Moreover, even the acquisition of an explanation may in itself add to self-esteem, since it increases one's sense of prediction and control. Thus when fundamentalists attribute events to God, they are gaining vicarious control over their situation.[39] Hence, attributions are likely to be an important element of the belief systems associated with a fundamentalist social identity, since they may satisfy the psychological needs which social identities serve. In particular, believers in the supernatural are likely to make attributions of causality to God and, perhaps, to Satan in certain circumstances.

The key task for researchers has been to specify what those circumstances are. What is it which prompts a religious or supernatural, rather than a secular or natural, explanation for an event? An important investigation attempting to answer this question is that of Lupfer and colleagues.[40] These investigators presented vignettes of common activities, some of them secular in content (e.g. exercising regularly) and others religious (e.g. supporting prayer in schools). Some of the vignettes presented examples of positively valued, others of negatively valued, behaviour. Their respondents were students who had identified themselves as fundamentalists by indicating beliefs in the supreme authority of the Bible, the experience of born-again conversion, the duty to evangelise, and socially conservative attitudes. God was invoked as the cause of the actions presented in the vignettes more often by the more fundamentalist respondents. Attributions to God were similarly more likely for the religious rather than the secular, and for the positive rather than the negative vignettes, and there was an interaction effect such that these differences were greater for the more fundamentalist respondents. Moreover, Satan was invoked more often by the more fundamentalist respondents, and was more likely to be held responsible for negative rather than positive events.

However, 90 per cent of the attributional explanations were secular rather than religious, even among a sample of respondents chosen for their fundamentalist beliefs. Lupfer and colleagues speculate as to the reasons for this huge preponderance of secular attributions. They ignore the most obvious, that is that people do not feel the need to seek for the cause of many events in their lives, but simply take them for granted. Many of their vignettes may have been sufficiently prosaic as not to require explanation. They dismiss the hypothesis that the secular explanation is, as it were, the default attribution, with religious attributions only occurring when secular ones seem inadequate, since there was no such correlation observed. On the basis of their evidence, there was no reason to suppose that religious explanations are reserved for unusual, important or emotionally charged events which are hard to account for in secular terms. Perhaps, they suggest, there are two levels of explanation: the immediate, or 'proximal', and the more general and remote, or 'distal'. God would be more likely to be invoked as being generally in control, whereas individuals or specific situations may be proposed as proximal explanations.

Other research, however, does support the notion of a 'God of the gaps' (i.e. events which are hard to explain are attributed to God). More attributions to God were found when the events presented were more important to respondents, and also when they were medical in nature rather than economic or social.[41] When respondents are given a more sophisticated set of alternative attributions to choose from, a more complex picture appears. Highly religious Australian Presbyterians attributed events most often to God allowing them to happen, followed in decreasing order of frequency by attributions to the self, to others, to God acting through people, to luck, and to God causing or controlling.[42] These results support the notion of a more distal form of attribution to God.[43,44]

These results may be interpreted in terms of SID. We may assume attributional beliefs to be part of the BVNs associated with a fundamentalist identity. Therefore they are likely to become salient in the adherent's mind for two reasons. First, the fundamentalist identity is central within, and of supreme importance for, the individual's self; and second, social situations frequently occur in which there are other members of the fundamentalist category present.

It is clear that the Protestant fundamentalist belief system may be characterised as a worldview in which there are two realms of reality: the natural order and the supernatural. God and other supernatural beings are assumed to exist in the supernatural sphere, but to intervene within the natural world. Indeed, God is believed by many Christian fundamentalists to rule over the world as Sovereign King already, not in some future kingdom.[45] Hence, on the basis of their doctrine, we would expect fundamentalist believers to make many more attributions to God than other believers, and many less to themselves. Evidence suggests that more fundamentalist believers are apt to adopt a 'deferring' mode of attribution to God; that is, they conceive of an active and intervening God, but of a passive believer.[46]

These attributions to the supernatural seem likely to serve the need for self-esteem as well as providing an over-arching worldview. For while one's successes may be attributed to God, at least one gains some reflected glory from being on His side; and one's failures are explicable in terms of the crafty wiles of the Devil. But there is still room for some more direct self-esteem. When respondents were requested to explain why they believed in God, they responded that their own beliefs were more internally and rationally based than were those of other believers and non-believers. Non-believers, however, did not credit themselves with being more rational than their fellow non-believers.[47]

The low self-esteem consequent upon feelings of sin, shame and guilt has long been seen as a likely outcome of Christian fundamentalist belief.[48] However, the dramatic Pauline conversion narrative favoured by fundamentalists induces such feelings only to relieve them immediately when the sinner accepts Christ as Saviour. Moreover, the strict rules of fundamentalist belief and practice, together with the threat of church discipline for those who break them, are not likely to induce such feelings either. On the contrary, the feeling of superiority over those who do not recognise and follow these rules will probably enhance the self-esteem of the overwhelming conformist majority. Consistent with this hypothesis is the finding that very fundamentalist believers rate themselves in general more highly than they rate other people, and that this effect is greater than for those who score low on the fundamentalism scale.[49]

The literature on attributions is compatible with hypothesis 13.

Cognitive complexity and rigidity

Considerable research effort has been expended on the apparent simplicity of the fundamentalist belief system. We would expect

simple systems, with dualistic features and clearly defined categories, to be more effective in reducing most people's uncertainty
than more complex theologies. Measures of complexity distinguish
two features: differentiation, which means the acknowledgement
of, and tolerance for, different perspectives; and integration, referring to the degree of linkage between these different perspectives.
The overall conclusion that has been drawn from this body of
research[50,51] is that fundamentalists are indeed less complex than
others, but that this lack of complexity obtains only in one particular area of belief, namely, existential beliefs.

Hunsberger and colleagues presented a set of issues to respondents differing on the fundamentalism scale. These related to
religious, ethical and environmental questions, and were either
familiar or unfamiliar to the respondents. Religious fundamentalism was only related to complexity of response for two of the six
dilemmas: how can belief in a loving God be reconciled with the
death of a believer's daughter in a car crash; and whether or not
abortion should be legalised. This selective lack of complexity was
explained in terms of the centrality of these beliefs within the
fundamentalist belief system. Any threat to these core beliefs is met
by simple affirmation. For example, in answer to the first of these
two dilemmas, a highly fundamentalist respondent replied: 'This is
entirely a question of faith. There is nothing else to find out about
the situation. It just comes with your faith . . . It says in the Bible
that God will not let anything happen to you that you can't handle.
So there has to be a reason for it'.[52]

Moreover, those scoring higher on the fundamentalism scale
express less doubts about their beliefs than do those scoring lower.
Further, those doubts which they do express tend to relate to other
people's failures, for example, the failure of other Christians to live
up to their ideals. It is the lower scorers who have doubts about
such fundamentals as the existence of God.[53] These latter doubts
can result in individuals leaving the faith in which they have been
brought up.[54]

The evidence regarding complexity of thought is consistent with
SID. The fundamentalist belief system consists at its core of a few
basic propositions (e.g. that the Bible is the inerrant Word of God).
Hence if these propositions are challenged, the social identity of
believer is threatened. No such doubts must be permitted to enter
the fundamentalist's mind, with the result that little questioning
occurs and therefore the belief stays simple (and very often

dualistic). On the other hand, many other beliefs are not considered basic and essential, and often are extremely complex (e.g. different positions on eschatology). It is the threat to the self which explains the simplicity of the existential beliefs, and their unwillingness to read anything which might challenge them.[55]

A related issue concerns the *rigidity* of such belief systems. In other words, how likely are fundamentalists to change their beliefs in the face of apparently conflicting evidence? In their classic study,[56] Festinger and colleagues examined what happens when the end of the world does not occur when predicted, or, as they put it, 'when prophecy fails'. They found that adherents maintained their beliefs subsequently, and redoubled their evangelising efforts. Festinger explained these findings in terms of the need to reduce cognitive dissonance. Another apparent example of rigidity relates to the Protestant fundamentalist refusal to accept the overwhelming scientific evidence for an evolutionary account of the development of the natural world in favour of a creationist or 'intelligent design' approach based on the Genesis myth (I use the term 'myth' to refer to a story with a profound meaning).

However, there are alternative explanations for this apparent refusal to confront the evidence which are more compatible with SID, and which do more justice to the internal logic and coherence of fundamentalist belief systems. What cannot possibly be entertained is the idea that God's Word is in any sense mistaken. For the inerrancy of scripture is one of the basic and non-negotiable beliefs which are the foundation of fundamentalist doctrine. If you regard the Bible as a historically accurate and scientifically sound account of events, then it becomes essential to defend what appears to the outsider to be indefensible.[57,58]

Thus an interpretation of these findings in terms of SID would stress that the basic elements of the BVNs which characterise the fundamentalist social identity are highly unlikely to change in the face of conflicting evidence. For that evidence is devised by 'the enemy', in other words, the secular world, and is to be interpreted as simply another attack on God's truth and on His faithful people who uphold it. A homogeneous and consistent set of BVNs is to be seen primarily as a means of reinforcing the conformity and cohesiveness of adherents, and of enabling them to distinguish themselves sharply from out-groups. Hence, the more apparently extreme and extraordinary their beliefs, the better these purposes are achieved. It is the social relations and consequent social identities which underpin the belief system which are important. Thus the literature on complexity and rigidity tends to support hypotheses 2, 4, 5, 11 and 12.

We may conclude on the basis of this brief and selective review of the social psychological research literature on fundamentalism that SID offers a promising alternative explanation for many of the findings. A theory which treats perceived membership of a category as the basis for a socially constructed self offers more explanatory power than approaches based on individual differences of religious orientation. SID generates a series of testable predictions which are certainly not inconsistent with the research evidence. In some areas of research, for example, those regarding sects and their attractiveness, and prejudicial attitudes, predictions derived from SID actually appear to offer a better account of the evidence than that proposed by existing theories. In the case of attributions and cognitive complexity and rigidity, the predictions from SID are at least not incompatible with the research results.

However, it must be admitted that the overall support to be derived from the existing research is slim, and therefore the next two chapters present case studies which may add some discursive weight. The commentary in these chapters is aimed at establishing that the cases do indeed both represent fundamentalisms in action. The subsequent chapter, Chapter 6, will seek to demonstrate that they are both well explained by SID.

Chapter 4

Mohammed Atta

A battle for the sake of God

Mohammed Atta, the operational leader of the attacks on the USA of 9/11 2001 and the pilot of the first plane to hit the World Trade Center, left two documents behind. The first was his last will and testament,[1] and the second a set of instructions to his accomplices.[2] It is not entirely certain who wrote the instructions. However, it is likely that it was Atta or one of his colleagues, since they contain the sentence: 'Afterwards, we will all meet in the highest heaven, God willing'.

Atta's will is typical of what one might expect of a pious Muslim. He writes, for example: 'I wanted the people who I left behind to hear God and not to be deceived by what life has to offer, and to pray more to God and to be good believers'. Perhaps its only unusual feature is its particular emphasis on the strict avoidance of women. 'I don't want a pregnant woman or a person who is not clean to come and say goodbye to me, because I don't approve it', he insists; 'I don't want women to come to my house to apologise for my death'. And, more strangely, 'The person who will wash my body near my genitals must wear gloves on his hands so he won't touch my genitals'. However, these instructions merely represent an exaggerated emphasis on Muslim traditions of purity. There is no indication in the will, which was written in 1996, that Atta expected imminent martyrdom in a war against infidels.

The instructions to the accomplices, however, are far more informative. They constitute a detailed sequence of actions to be taken on the night of 10 September, and on the fateful day itself. This document could hardly be more religious in its tone and content.[3] There are 89 references to God, and 25 to the Prophet

Mohammed. The religious topics of ritual purification, martyrdom and its rewards and the struggle against infidels are referred to regularly. The importance of praying to God at every stage of the operation is emphasised. Traditional prophylactic prayers for times of the day, for entry into new surroundings such as the taxi or the plane, for battle and for the moment of death are enjoined. And the Qur'ān is frequently quoted verbatim (on 22 occasions), or alluded to. Throughout, religious belief and its practical application in action are so closely intertwined as to be indistinguishable. Every act is suffused with spirituality. The word and the deed are one.

There is therefore no question that, from the writer's perspective at the very least, the actions of 9/11 were replete with religious meaning and had a religious motive and justification. Since the writer felt that these instructions would inspire his accomplices as well, it is reasonable to assume that they were similar believers. The assault on the symbols of American power was, the author believed, his sacred duty. It is clear from the document that the defining features of fundamentalism are nearly all present and dominant in the thinking of its author.[4] Mohammed Atta, if it was he, was a fundamentalist.

First, the document is permeated with the idea of religion as a *reaction* against a hostile secularism. One of the first instructions is: 'Make sure you know all aspects of the plan well, and expect the response, or a reaction, from the enemy'. The victims of the attack are construed as 'the enemy'. Atta's accomplices are urged to 'Pray during the night, and be persistent in asking God to give you victory, control, and conquest, and that He may make your task easier and not expose us'. This is war, the ultimate reaction against those perceived as hostile. Immediately, this construction is rammed home. The accomplices are first urged to read Chapters 8 and 9 of the Qur'ān, entitled 'The Spoils' and 'Repentance'. These are traditional war chapters, Chapter 8 referring to the victory of the Prophet at the Battle of Sadr, AD 624. One verse reads: 'When the sacred months are over, slay the idolators wherever you find them. Arrest them, besiege them, and lie in ambush everywhere for them. If they repent and take to prayer and pay the alms tax, let them go their way. Allah is forgiving and merciful'.[5]

War means violence, but the violence is entirely justified, for it is God's will.[6] The enemy is the infidel, the secular world, all who do not obey God's law, but rather seek to destroy it. War is therefore essential, since otherwise the existence of God's people is threatened. War is their only hope, and compromise is impossible. The struggle is cosmic; two entirely different worldviews are in conflict. The two sets of combatants' weapons of war are therefore incomparable. The enemy fights with all the power of modern technology, the faithful with faith and knives: the material versus the spiritual, Satan versus God. The second defining feature of fundamentalism, *dualism*, is clearly evident here. Atta reassures his colleagues:

> All of their equipment and gates and technology will not prevent, nor harm, except by God's will. The believers do not fear such things. The only ones that fear it are the allies of Satan, who are the brothers of the Devil . . . He [*God*] said in the verses: 'This is only the Devil scaring his allies' who are fascinated with Western civilisation.

Ironically, the passengers who resisted fought back with their penknives.

Atta has no doubt that the enemy will fight back, in accord with his aims to destroy God's faithful. When Atta's colleagues are in the plane:

> this is the moment that both groups come together. So remember God, as he said in His book: 'Oh Lord, pour your patience upon us, and make our feet steadfast, and give us victory over the infidels.' And His prophet said: 'Oh Lord, You have revealed the book You move the clouds, You gave us victory over the enemy, conquer them and give us victory over them.' Give us victory, and make the ground shake under their feet. Pray for yourself and all your brothers, that they may be victorious and hit their targets, and ask God to give you martyrdom facing the enemy, not running away from him, and for Him to grant you patience and the feeling that anything that happens to you is for Him.

Atta makes it clear to his accomplices that the victims are not theirs but God's. The passengers are not to be killed as an act of personal revenge, but solely because it is God's will that they should die. 'Do not seek revenge for yourself', he commands, 'Strike for God's sake. Make sure your soul is prepared to do everything for God only'. He tells his followers to avoid causing discomfort to those they are killing, for this is in accord with the Prophet's practice. However, the Prophet took no prisoners, and nor should they: 'Take prisoners and kill them. As Almighty God said: "No prophet should have prisoners until he has soaked the land with blood"'.

The dualism between this present evil world and the world of the spirit is nowhere more clearly expressed than in the document's repeated promises of the rewards of martyrdom. The entire operation is framed within the ritual of sacrifice. The accomplices are told to 'shave excess hair from the body and wear cologne. Shower . . . Purify your soul from all unclean things. Completely forget something called "this world"'. They are instructed to tighten their clothes, possibly in order to make sure that they will cover their genitals at all times. To be seen uncovered would render them impure, and not an acceptable sacrifice in a proper state of ablution. They:

> should feel complete tranquillity, because the time between you and your marriage is very short. Afterwards begins the happy life, where God is satisfied with you, and eternal bliss 'in the company of the prophets, the companions, the martyrs, and the good people, who are all good company'.

However, in a passage which featured strongly in media accounts, Atta suggests that the rewards may not be entirely spiritual: 'Know that the gardens of paradise are waiting for you in all their beauty, and the women of paradise are waiting, calling out "Come hither, friend of God". They have dressed in their most beautiful clothing'.

The third distinctive feature of fundamentalism is the appeal to *authority*, especially that of the holy book. Atta's instructions constantly reaffirm the total authority of God, whose will is made clear in His word the Qur'ān, and interpreted by the Prophet and others: 'Remember God frequently, and the best way to do it is to read the Holy Qur'ān, according to all the scholars, as far as I know. It is enough for us that it is the words of the Creator of the Earth and the plants, the One that you will meet'.

The document's readers are reminded repeatedly of 'the words of Almighty God', or that 'Almighty God said'. These passages refer to the words of the Qur'ān, which is assumed to be the means whereby God directly expresses his will. The holy book has such power that it can work miracles: Atta tells his accomplices to 'Bless your body with some verses of the Qur'ān [accomplished by reading some verses into one's cupped hands, and then rubbing the hands over whatever is to be blessed], the luggage, clothes, the knife, your personal effects, your ID, passport, and all your papers'. Even the very letters of the Arabic text carry power: 'Whoever thinks deeply about these words [the Qur'ān text "there is no God but Allah"] will find that they have no dots and this is just one of its greatnesses, for words that have dots in them carry less weight than those that do not'.

The authority of God's word is supported by frequent invocations of the Prophet and his immediate followers. Atta seeks to bring in aid the mythical heroes of the faith to boost his twentieth-century fundamentalist movement. For example:

> Then every one of you should prepare to carry out his role in a way that would satisfy God. You should clench your teeth, as the pious early generations did . . . sing songs to boost morale, as the pious first generations did in the throes of battle, to bring calm tranquillity and joy to the hearts of his brothers.

Finally, at the very end of the document, the hijackers are encouraged to identify with these heroes:

> If you see the enemy as strong, remember the groups [the enemies of the Prophet]. They were 10,000. Remember how God gave victory to his faithful servants. He said 'When the faithful saw the groups, they said, this is what God and the Prophet promised, they said the truth. It only increased their faith'.

And Atta finally signs off, 'And may the peace of God be upon the Prophet'.

Of course, these quotations and examples from history and from the Qur'ān are highly *selective*, the fourth distinguishing feature of fundamentalisms. Ancient texts are treated as direct communications from the Almighty to today's faithful. Atta does not take the Qur'ān as a whole and in its historical context. He does not derive a theology from such a reading, which would undoubtedly give pride of place to a vision of a God who required justice for the poor, tolerance and compassion.[7] Rather, like all fundamentalists from Judaism, Islam and Christianity, the three major 'religions of the book', he picks out specific passages, or even mere verses, which support his purposes. Thus the two chapters selected to be read by his accomplices are the traditional war chapters. Each subsequent quotation is selected so that it appears to justify or enjoin the specific action which he is instructing them to take. The battles of the seventh century are transposed to the twenty-first, and the hijacking is glorified as 'a battle for the sake of God'.

The fifth and final defining feature of fundamentalisms, a strong *millennialist emphasis* on the last days, is absent from the document. This is not surprising, since in his will Atta describes himself as a Sunni Muslim. While apocalypse is present in Shi'ite Muslim belief,[8] it is of lesser importance to Sunnis. It is not surprising, however, that apocalyptic imagery dominated reportage of 9/11 in the American media, as millennialism is certainly central to American Protestant fundamentalism.[9]

We may conclude, then, that the hijackers were fundamentalists. They clearly fulfilled four of the five criteria for being categorised as such.

The formation of a fundamentalist

How then did a relatively secular middle-class Egyptian boy become the pious Muslim who made his will at the age of 28, and then morph into the 33-year-old hijacker who destroyed the twin towers in 2001? Or, to use the astounded words of the wife of Atta's flatmate, how did 'little Mohammed in the blue flip-flops' turn into a revolutionary commander?[10]

Those who prefer the Pauline conversion account of personal change try to find a turning point in Atta's life story. We want the story to be St Paul's conversion in reverse: a good middle-class boy just like the rest of us is suddenly transformed by evil forces into a monster. However, there seems to be little evidence of any such 'road to Damascus' experience. Perhaps we need the myth because we cannot conceive of the possibility that many thousands of intelligent and educated people can be radicalised by their experiences into becoming fundamentalist political activists. Indeed, it seems likely from what little we know about him that Mohammed Atta underwent just such a gradual radicalisation.

He was born in 1968, the youngest of three children, to a self-made and ambitious Egyptian lawyer. His father drove his children hard to achieve academically, and Mohammed's older sisters became a doctor and a university teacher. The family were not regular attenders at their mosque, and when Mohammed went on to Cairo University in 1985 he was not noted for being particularly political or religious. However, he was a member of the Engineering Faculty, a stronghold of the relatively radical Muslim Brotherhood, and so must have been exposed to some radical ideas. Furthermore, the secular government of President Mubarak was cracking down hard on its fundamentalist opponents, who were plotting against it.

Atta was unable to undertake postgraduate study in Cairo because his undergraduate academic performance was not good enough, so he went with his father's blessing to study in Hamburg. As soon as he arrived there, he started to attend the mosque daily for worship, to fast and to pray five times a day. He was not observed to take part in worldly pleasures. In other words, he started taking his religion seriously. He told his landlady, apropos of another matter: 'I'm abroad now; I'm grown up. Now I can decide on my own'. It is possible that his new distance from his father enabled him to do what he had wanted to do for some time. As to his motivation for his new religious zeal, we can only guess. It may be that he was radicalised into fundamentalism to a certain extent at Cairo University, but hesitated to practise his faith overtly because his father had warned him against political/religious involvement.

A more personal reason to embrace a moralistic faith might have been his ambivalent attitude towards sex. He is reported to have done the following: walked out of the room as a teenager when belly dancing was shown on television; been offended by his landlady's bare arms in Hamburg; asked for a nude by Degas to be taken off the wall of his student lodgings; withdrawn from help with his thesis because it involved close physical proximity to his female helper;[11] and refused to shake hands with the female examiner of his thesis. Taken together with the remarks about women in his will (see p. 57), these reports might indicate the psychological processes of denial of sexuality and reaction formation, for which stern religion is an appropriate vehicle.

All this is speculative. What is for sure is that soon after arriving in Hamburg he changed his degree course from architecture to urban planning, and began to specialise in the preservation of old Islamic cities. When he undertook practical projects in this topic in Aleppo, Syria, and back home in Cairo, what he discovered made him very angry. Old Islamic districts were being transformed into theme parks for tourists, with local Muslims losing their livelihoods and their traditional way of life.

In 1995 he undertook the pilgrimage to Mecca, one of the sacred duties of the practising Muslim. Or at least, he is reported to have done so. A Protestant German fellow student says that he never talked about this pilgrimage, even though they often engaged in religious discussions. When he returned from Mecca, or from wherever it was he went, he is reported to have become more fervent in his religiosity, and to have indicated fear of suffering political persecution in Egypt. He also started attending Al Quds mosque, the most radical mosque in Hamburg.

Having completed the taught part of his postgraduate degree, he began to write up his thesis in 1997. He was seen little at the university, although he periodically gave some postgraduate seminars. There are two months at the beginning of 1998 when he could have gone abroad. He himself said he had gone on another pilgrimage, but some believe he was receiving training to become a terrorist. It is clear that he left his student lodgings at this time and moved, first into a housing project and then into a rented flat. Many Arabs visited him in the housing project, while at the flat expensive computer equipment was installed. His two fellow tenants in the flat, Ramzi Binalshibh and Said Bahaji, would both leave the flat suddenly shortly before the 9/11 attacks. Among the frequent Arab visitors were two men who were among the hijackers.

However, it does not follow that Atta was already at this time plotting with others to attack America by plane. On the contrary, there are indications that this fateful step was not yet in their plans or their imagination. Atta finished his thesis and got his degree. His pious dedication on its first page was a verse of the Qur'ān which reads as follows: 'Say "My prayer and my sacrifice and my life and my death are for Allah, the Lord of the Worlds"'. He returned to Cairo during 1999, where he found his mother to be ill. He is reported to have wished to stay to take care of her.

However, he was now sufficiently radicalised to have joined three colleagues in travelling to Afghanistan seeking training to fight in the rebel cause in Chechnya. They did not achieve their wish. By early 2000, the four had been sent back to Hamburg to get visas, go to the USA and learn to fly. For the 9/11 plot was not their idea, but that of a much bigger fish in the militant pond, Khaled Sheikh Mohammed.[12]

A few radical Islamists had become disillusioned by their failure to mobilise successful revolutions in nominally Muslim countries such as Egypt. They decided instead to carry out assaults on America, the Great Satan. But how could they penetrate its defences? Sheikh Mohammed had long wanted to destroy passenger jets. Late in 1996 he had presented to Osama bin Laden his idea of hijacking planes in America and crashing them into the CIA and FBI headquarters, the tallest buildings on the East and West Coasts of America, and nuclear power plants. Early in 1999, bin Laden, having successfully attacked American embassies in Africa, finally gave the go-ahead. However, the four operatives allocated to the task either failed to get visas or could not speak English. Then four young educated English-speaking Arabs turned up in Afghanistan, and the rest is history.

Atta has consistently been referred to by those who knew him as a very limited person. He was certainly single-minded, thorough, resolute and disciplined. But he seemed insulated against the outside world, locked up within himself and incapable of forming relationships. Technically competent, he lacked imagination and flair. He was, therefore, just the sort of good soldier to carry out the horribly imaginative plans of others. He could render the horrific banal, as happened in the Holocaust. But then, drawing upon his fundamentalist faith, he could clothe the banal in religious fervour.

But how could he produce that extraordinary set of instructions for his fellow conspirators? What were the ideological origins of his perception of Islam? These can only be understood by a closer look at the ideas of two of the ideologists of radical Islam which informed his religious development: Abu Ala Mawdudi (1903–79) and Sayyid Qutb (1906–66).

Jahiliyaah and Jihad

Both Mawdudi and Qutb lived in recently secularised nationalist states, Mawdudi in India and then Pakistan, Qutb in Egypt. Both suffered persecution, Mawdudi as a Muslim in a predominantly Hindu country, Qutb as an alleged plotter against the Muslim

President Nasser. Indeed, Qutb was imprisoned for ten years and then executed. Both men were so formed by their experience that they responded with a classic fundamentalist reactivity. They perceived the world in dualist terms, claimed authority from God and the Qur'ãn, but used the latter selectively to justify their ideology. Both were prime examples of fundamentalism.

Mawdudi was a truly revolutionary ideologue. He was convinced that those Muslims such as the Muslim Brotherhood, who had sought accommodation with the West while trying to protect the faith, had failed. He therefore sought to formulate an ideology which expressed the difference between faith and secularism in the starkest possible terms. At the same time, he needed to mobilise action by the faithful against the newly-defined and demonised enemy. However, any revolutionary formulations of the faith still had to be buttressed and justified by reference to God's word.

He first established as strong a contrast as he possibly could between the faith and its secular enemy. This he did by defining the faith in terms of God's rule. It is God who is sovereign over human affairs, he affirmed, and it is his Law, the Sharia, which should regulate them. All who reject such a theocratic form of government are in thrall to the enemy. They obey mere human laws, and are in fact in slavery to those who wield political power. They can only become truly free by rejecting their human leaders and submitting themselves to the sovereignty of God. Otherwise they are still enslaved by the *jahiliyaah*, the ignorant and brutish barbarism of the West. Mawdudi had transformed the original reference of this idea to those alive before the Prophet's ministry to apply to the present day secular enemy.

Having sharply distinguished the protagonists, Mawdudi's next revolutionary task was to set up the struggle itself. To this end he picked up the theological concept of *jihad*, and enthroned it as the central tenet of the faith. He selected the sacred saying 'I have been ordered to fight people until they say "There is no God but Allah". If they say it, they have protected their blood, their wealth from me. Their recompense is with God'. Commenting on this, Mawdudi asserts:

> Islam wants the whole earth and does not content itself with being only a part thereof. It wants and requires the entire inhabited world. It does not want this in order that one nation dominates the earth and monopolises its sources of wealth,

after having taken them away from one or more other nations. No, Islam wants and requires the earth in order that the human race altogether can enjoy the concept and practical program of human happiness, by means of which God has honoured Islam and put it above the other religions and laws. In order to realise this lofty desire, Islam wants to employ all forces and means that can be employed for bringing about a universal all-embracing revolution. It will spare no efforts for the achievement of this supreme objective. This far-reaching struggle that continuously exhausts all forces and this employment of all possible means are called *Jihad*.[13]

By prioritising the concept of *jihad* in this way, Mawdudi superceded the five pillars of Islam: the testimony of faith; prayer; the giving of alms; fasting; and making the pilgrimage.[14] The concept had previously served to emphasise the commitment which was needed to be steadfast in the faith and to defend it against its enemies. Mawdudi transformed it to serve instead the idea of revolutionary struggle. The Muslim teaching that only defensive wars were justified was discarded, since it did not meet his ideological needs. Anyway, the revolution can be represented as a defensive war against the onslaught of secularism. As with the concept of *jahiliyaah*, so with *jihad*: the holy writings were selectively adapted to suit the author's purpose.

Mawdudi confidently deals with the paradox of freedom within a theocratic state:

> Islamic *jihad* does not seek to interfere with the faith, ideology, rituals of worship or social customs of the people. It allows them perfect freedom of religious belief and permits them to act according to their creed. However, Islamic *jihad* does not recognise their right to administer state affairs according to a system which, in the view of Islam, is evil. Furthermore, Islamic *jihad* also refuses to admit their right to continue with such practices under an Islamic government which fatally affect the public interest from the viewpoint of Islam.[15]

In other words, true freedom is only possible under the rule of God's law. Thus, whatever each of the two adversaries in the struggle believes to be freedom, the other perceives as servitude.

Sayyid Qutb developed this revolutionary ideology further. He maintained Mawdudi's dualistic opposition of the sovereignty of God to that of man. He wrote in his book *Milestones*:

> This religion is really a universal declaration of the freedom of man from servitude to other men and from servitude to their own desires, which is also a form of human servitude; it is a declaration that sovereignty belongs to God alone and that he is the Lord of all the worlds. It means a challenge to all kinds and forms of systems which are based on the concept of the sovereignty of man; in other words, where man has usurped the Divine attribute. Any system in which the final decisions are referred to human beings, and in which the sources of all authority are human, deifies human beings by designating others than God as lords over men. This declaration means that the usurped authority of God be returned to him, and the usurpers be thrown out – those who by themselves devise laws for others to follow, thus elevating themselves to the status of lords and reducing others to the status of slaves. In short, to proclaim the authority and sovereignty of God means to eliminate all human kingship and to announce the rule of the Sustainer of the Universe over the entire earth. In the words of the Qur'ān: 'He alone is God in the heavens and in the earth'.[16]

Qutb returns repeatedly to his argument that establishing universal Islamic government over people in no way damages their freedom of belief. Once the law of God has been imposed, people will be free to believe and practise their religion as they wish. Paradoxically, conquest sets up the conditions for freedom. To quote:

> this religion forbids the imposition of its belief by force, as is clear from the verse 'there is no compulsion in religion' (Qur'ān 2: 256), while on the other hand it tries to annihilate all those political and material powers which stand between people and Islam, which force one people to bow before another people, and prevent them from accepting the sovereignty of God. These two principles have no relation to one another, nor is there room to mix them . . . Thus, wherever an Islamic community exists which is a concrete example of the Divinely-ordained system of life, it has a God-given right to

step forward and take control of the political authority so that it may establish the Divine system on earth, while it leaves the matter of belief to individual conscience.[17]

Qutb further extended the concept of *jahiliyaah*, used to describe the enemy. He takes it to include all secular systems:

> The *jahili* society is any society other than the Muslim society; and if we want a more specific definition, we may say that any society is a *jahili* society which does not dedicate itself to submission to God alone, in its beliefs and ideas, in its observances of worship, and in its legal regulations. According to this definition, all the societies existing in the world today are *jahili*.[18]

He goes on to spell out the fact that this definition includes communists, Christians, Jews, and 'idolators', and even Muslim states:

> We classify them among *jahili* societies not because they believe in other deities beside God, nor because they worship anyone other than God, but because their way of life is not based on submission to God alone. Although they believe in the Unity of God, still they have relegated the legislative attribute of God to others and submit to this authority, and from this authority they derive their systems, their traditions and customs, their laws, their values and standards, and almost every practice of life.[19]

Thus Qutb extended the scope of *jihad* to include nations such as Egypt itself, in whose prison he was incarcerated. He even justified the assassination of a ruler of a secular Muslim nation by arguing that he was not really a Muslim, thereby signing his own death warrant. He also developed the idea of *jihad* by spelling out its methodology. In true fundamentalist fashion, he appropriated the stages of the life and work of the Prophet, and applied them to the revolutionary vanguard of believers (*jamaah*) who would spearhead *jihad*. These four stages are in fact the 'milestones' of his book title. First, the vanguard group must separate itself out from its *jahili* environment. Second, it should create a pure Muslim enclave, which in the third stage becomes an Islamic state. From this third stage, the vanguard could launch into the final stage of armed struggle, just as the Prophet had engaged in raids against Mecca. And the result will be, now as it was then, the acceptance of the rule of Islam and the sovereignty of God.

Perhaps it was his own parlous position in prison and the failure of various attempts to overthrow President Nasser which prompted Qutb's final development of fundamentalist revolutionary Islam: the doctrine of superiority. Qutb argues, again paradoxically, that what appears to be failure to secular perceptions is to be construed by the faithful as success, and indeed superiority. Defeat is really triumph. When two worldviews are entirely opposite, it is hardly surprising that the same concept has opposite meanings. Chapter 11 of *Milestones* is entitled 'The Faith Triumphant', and is prefaced by a verse from the Qur'ān[20] which reads:

> 'Do not be dejected nor grieve. You shall be the uppermost if you are believers'. This verse means to feel superior to others when weak, few, and poor, as well as when many and rich. For God does not leave the believer alone in the face of oppression to whimper under its weight, to suffer dejection and grief, but relieves them of all this with the message: Do not be dejected [etc.]. This message relieves him from both dejection and grief, these two feelings being natural for a human being in this situation. It relieves him of both, not merely through patience and steadfastness, but also through a sense of superiority from whose heights the power of oppression, the dominant values, the current concepts, the standards, the rules, the customs and habits, and the people steeped in error, all seem low.[21]

The people steeped in error certainly seemed low to Qutb himself, as he years earlier spent an unhappy two years in America as an education official of the Egyptian government: 'The American girl is well acquainted with her body's seductive capacity. She knows it lies in the face, and in expressive eyes and thirsty lips. She knows seductiveness lies in the round breasts, the full buttocks, and in the shapely thighs, sleek legs – and she knows all this and does not hide it'. As for the American male: 'This primitiveness can be seen in the spectacle of the fans as they follow a game of football, or watch boxing matches or bloody, monstrous wrestling matches . . . This spectacle leaves no room for doubt as to the primitiveness of the feelings of those who are enamoured with muscular strength and desire it.[22]

The believer can certainly feel superior to these degraded creatures:

> He is most superior in his conscience and understanding, in his morals and manners, as he believes in God who has excellent names and attributes. This by itself creates in him a sense of dignity, purity and cleanliness, modesty and piety, and a desire for good deeds and of being a rightly-guided representative of God on earth. Furthermore, this belief gives him the assurance that the reward is in the Hereafter, the reward before which the troubles of the world and all its sorrows become insignificant. The heart of the believer is content with it, although he may pass through this life without apparent success.[23]

So a feeling of spiritual and moral superiority transforms what the secular world would regard as failure into success, a success which will be crowned by eternal spiritual rewards in heaven. A martyr's death is the ultimate example of true spiritual success:

> Conditions change, the Muslim loses his physical power and is conquered, yet the consciousness does not depart from him that he is the most superior. If he remains a Believer, he looks upon his conqueror from a superior position. He remains certain that this is a temporary condition which will pass away and that faith will turn the tide from which there is no escape. Even if death is his portion, he will never bow his head. Death comes to all, but for him there is martyrdom. He will proceed to the Garden, while his conquerors go to the Fire. What a difference!.[24]

These revolutionary concepts of fundamentalist Islam, derived from Mawdudi and Qutb, permeate the instructions which Atta wrote for his co-conspirators. They also even permeate his character and habits. His character, his action, and his fundamentalist beliefs are all of a piece. We find echoes of Qutb in the emphasis on Atta's steadfastness, single-mindedness and absolute devotion to his religion described in others' accounts of him. The sense of superiority over others, particularly in terms of sexual and ritual purity, is clear, both in Atta's life and in the instructions. Qutb's emphasis on apparent weakness as a source of strength is also repeated in the instructions, particularly in those passages where western technology is contrasted with the hijackers' faith. The instructions are steeped in the extreme reactive characterisations of others as the enemy, and in the dualism between the values of this ungodly world and those of the next, both typical of Mawdudi and Qutb. The whole document follows closely the typical fundamentalist method of textual exegesis, whereby stories or verses of the holy book are taken from their context and used to prefigure and justify the writer's argument.[25] The founding fathers of the faith are called in aid repeatedly to provide support for parts of the hijackers' plan, just as Qutb used the stages of the Prophet's life to support the formation of the revolutionary vanguard. And it is as members of that vanguard, who are to enjoy the rewards of martyrdom, that the hijackers are addressed by Atta.

Triumph and tragedy

So Mohammed Atta and his band of hijackers completed their dreadful task successfully. They were good soldiers and good revolutionary Muslims. Their fundamentalist religion had informed, motivated and justified their every action. They treated the operation as their sacred duty. But what of those who sent them on their mission? What did they hope to achieve, and did they too succeed?

The destruction of the twin towers was a global media event. It was a huge symbolic triumph for the small group who saw themselves as the global revolutionary vanguard of militant Islam.[26] They had successfully assaulted the very emblems of secularism, deep in the heartland of that bastion of secularism and modernity, America. (Actually, by some measures, America is the second most religious nation in the world!)[27] What is more, they had achieved their aim without compromising their purity. They had pitted their world of faith and knives against the world of secularism and high technology, and they had won. Moreover, they had brought fundamentalist religion to the very forefront of the world's attention, and shown that it could be victorious in the cosmic struggle between God and Satan, good and evil.

But they also achieved another important objective: to get their definition of geopolitics accepted by their victims. The world was now at war. Of course, the very audacity of their assault made it politically imperative for the American government to respond in a vigorous and aggressive way. However, it would still have been possible to characterise the plotters as a homicidal criminal group, thereby depriving them of the status of number one enemy of the West, which they craved.

President Bush, however, reinforced the plotters' definition of the situation as a cosmic war between good and evil. Bush's war was to be against 'terror', and it was to be fought by the citadel of 'freedom and democracy' and its allies. Thus he responded in a classical fundamentalist fashion to the fundamentalist threat. He was reactive against perceived threat and he construed the situation in dualistic and moralistic terms. Nevertheless, his response was not overtly religious. Rather, it is likely that his faith affected his response in several more indirect ways. First, since reactivity and dualism are two of the five distinctive features of fundamentalisms, they come naturally to a 'born-again' Christian. Second, despite the attempt by the founding fathers enshrined in the constitution to disassociate religion from the state, the idea of America as a nation especially favoured by God has always been deeply embedded in American culture. America is a city on a hill, a beacon of light for other nations, with a mission to share its blessings with the rest of the world. Third, Bush felt himself to be called and appointed by God to his office.[28] Hence an assault on America and its president was in effect an assault on God. Fourth, most American Protestant fundamentalists strongly favour Israel, and Bush was not only one of them but also depended on their votes. Finally, Protestant fundamentalism had itself been growing more militant at that time. While the moral majority of the 1980s had concentrated on fighting American secularists, more recently the Reformist theologians of the Reconstructionist movement had been aiming to conquer the world for God. In an eerie echo of Mawdudi and Qutb, they wished to establish global theocratic rule by God's law.[29]

Thus Bush's own beliefs made his declaration of a 'war against terror' more likely. His subsequent prosecution of that 'war', including the fighting of two real wars, was probably exactly what the plotters wanted and expected. They could easily portray his invasion of Arab nations as the persecution of Islam in general, and his use of such phrases as 'axis of evil' and 'crusade' gave credence to such a portrayal. He and the American military even sought to trump the assault on the twin towers by the 'shock and awe' bombing of Baghdad.

So the plotters had got what they wanted.[30] They had brought religion to the secular world's notice. They had shown themselves capable of attacking the heart of the secular world. They had set up a symbiotic relationship with that world by provoking a violent reaction to their own reactive and dualistic worldview. They had succeeded in establishing a climate of fear. And, finally, they had attracted thousands more would-be Mohammed Attas to the cause of revolutionary Islam.

Chapter 5

Angry Anglicans

The Anglicans

The Church of England famously came into being in the sixteenth
century as a consequence of King Henry VIII's need for a son and
heir.[1] But the notably uxorious monarch was but the surface reason
for the birth of this particular branch of the Protestant Church. The
underlying cause was the Reformation, that huge paradigm shift in
worldview which convulsed Europe for a century and more. It put
the Bible, the word of God, into the hands of an increasingly
educated laity, and invited it into a direct and personal experience
of God. The individual was saved by the grace of God; he or she
was chosen, and had only to accept God's gift of salvation by faith
and be converted. Salvation through observation of religious
rituals, obeying Mother Church, or performing good works was not
possible. The Roman Catholic Church's emphasis on the priest as
mediating between God and the community, and the spiritual and
temporal power of the Church as the controlling hub of the lives of
a largely rural people, were both challenged as never before.

In England, Archbishop Cranmer gave the stern continental
Reformist Puritanism of Luther and Calvin a gentler tone. He
created one of the jewels of Anglicanism, the Prayer Book of 1549,
revised in 1552, which contains such gems as the Collect for Purity:
'Almighty God, unto whom all hearts are open, all desires known,
and from whom no secrets are hid: Cleanse the thoughts of our
hearts by the inspiration of thy Holy Spirit that we may perfectly
love thee, and worthily magnify thy holy name; through Christ our
Lord. Amen'. The Catholics and the Calvinists both disapproved
of the Prayer Book, thus forming the pattern of a moderate centre
trying to hold together two extremist wings which was to continue

to the present day. Soon one or the other wing was to hold political and spiritual sway. Thomas Cromwell destroyed the monasteries in the space of about three years, and the Reformist Evangelicals who flourished under King Edward VI continued the persecution of Catholics. The boot was soon on the other foot when Queen Mary sought to return to the Roman Church, and made many Protestant martyrs, including Cranmer.

During the reign of Queen Elizabeth I, the moderate middle way was firmly re-established, and its theological foundations were identified as scripture, tradition and reason, thus including the Reformation, the historic Church, and a foretaste of the Enlightenment. This inclusive umbrella would, in the long run, survive both the Calvinistic Puritanism of Oliver Cromwell's revolution and the incipient Catholicism of the Restoration of the monarchy under the Stuart kings. It proved ideal for the eighteenth century, but failed to adapt rapidly enough to the Industrial Revolution, the migration to the cities and the growth of the urban proletariat. The evangelical wing, partly in the guise of the Methodists, gained influence in the late eighteenth and nineteenth centuries. However, this temporary supremacy was in no way hostile to the Enlightenment. On the contrary, evangelicals were eager to gain the benefits of education, and used it to further their knowledge of the world and their political and religious clout. A counterblast came from the Catholic wing in the 1830s, with the Oxford Movement under Keble and Pusey seeking to restore the importance of the liturgy and moderate what they saw as the excesses of the Reformation. But by the early twentieth century, the moderate middle had regained its dominance and, with the help of such outstanding archbishops as William Temple, retained it until well after the Second World War.

Without doubt, the position of the Anglicans as the established national Church strengthened the arm of the moderate middle, since in some sense the Church had to be representative of the nation and the varied historical strands of belief within it. So dominant was the middle in the first part of the twentieth century that the two wings had to join forces to achieve objectives which they shared for very different reasons. For example, the revised Prayer Book was voted down by an alliance of smells, bells and the metaphorical odour of sanctity in 1928. But, in a splendidly typical Anglican compromise, those who wished carried on and used it anyway.

After the Second World War, however, the centre started to come under renewed pressure, mostly from the evangelical wing. Transatlantic developments in American Protestantism were being exported to Britain in the 1950s, with the revivalist preaching of Billy Graham filling arenas across the nation and resulting in a new breed of convert. The cultural revolution of the 1960s had two consequences, both of which favoured the evangelicals. The first was the inevitable moral backlash, which in America took the form of the so-called moral majority of the 1980s and the selection of a relatively few moral issues to fight for. The second was the 1960s emphasis on individual emotionality and exploration and fulfilment of the self, which found its expression in ecstatic charismatic forms of worship. These two outcomes were evidenced in America by a huge growth in the Southern Baptist and Pentecostal churches,[2] which respectively represented the Calvinistic and the charismatic tendencies. These united to form a moral conservative movement, the Christian Right, for which the label 'majority' was only a slight exaggeration.[3] At the same time, the Episcopalians (the American branch of the Anglican Church) and the United Methodists, who both represented a more liberal theology, were losing members.

At this point a clarification and definition of terms is required. The labels 'evangelical' and 'fundamentalist' need careful consideration. Confusions in terminology have their origins in two different levels of explanation. The first relates to the cultural and religious histories of America and Britain. In America, the use of the self-descriptive term 'fundamentalist' preceded that of 'evangelical', at least when used of a doctrinal grouping. American Protestants first called themselves fundamentalists in the 1920s. The upsurge of evangelism in the 1950s, and the willingness of evangelists such as Billy Graham to collaborate with the mainstream churches, meant that many fundamentalists were hostile to these new, more 'liberal' evangelicals. It was only in the 1980s that the two groups collaborated, to form the 'moral majority'. In Britain, however, the label evangelical had long been used to describe the reformed wing of the Anglican Church. The term fundamentalist has been little used in Britain until the last two decades, and certainly does not have the same reference to a specific doctrinal group with a historical origin as it does in America.

The second level of explanation for our terminological distinctions addresses the criteria which we use for allocating labels for groups. In the previous paragraph, the assumption has been that we should use the terms which Christians have adopted for themselves, and which historians and commentators on religion have been happy to accept. Many scholars would argue that this is the only possible way to proceed, since we need to try to understand religious people's beliefs from their own perspective, and the way they label and define themselves is a major element of that perspective. However, there is a traditional social scientific alternative. It is to apply labels on the basis of the criteria which we have established for the use of terms. In Chapter 1 I outlined five definitive features of fundamentalism, implying that the term should be used only for religious movements which demonstrated those features, and that it should be used for all such movements. Clearly, therefore, the term should not be limited to a particular doctrinal group of Christians.

The term 'evangelical', on the other hand, does not have a specific social scientific definition. As a consequence, I will use it in this book as a culturally determined label, so that in fact it has different connotations in different cultures (Britain and America). The important point to make, therefore, is that some of those culturally defined as 'evangelicals' can also be defined as fundamentalists from a social scientific perspective. Of course, this is not to assume that the social scientific perspective is superior; social science, too, is a specific culture. Rather, it simply reminds the reader that this book is written from a social science perspective for social scientists. After all of which, it should be clear that the term evangelical as used in this chapter refers to the British use, but that many American evangelicals can be categorised as fundamentalists.

After the post-war boost to evangelical fortunes in Britain, the moderate heart of the Anglican Church, personified by Archbishop Runcie, was having difficulty in keeping its central position of power. Runcie encountered the most conservative British premier for years in Margaret Thatcher and suffered the inevitable bruises from his battering by the prime ministerial handbag. In a period of overall decline in Church membership and attendance, the evangelicals suffered less than other Anglicans. Less than a million regularly attend church out of some 26 million who say that they are 'C of E'.[4] By way of contrast, the Anglican Communion worldwide was growing fast, especially in Africa, where the vast majority of clergy and lay people were on the evangelical wing of the Church. Thus the evangelicals were growing in power and confidence.

Runcie was succeeded by Carey, who was an evangelical. He initiated a decade of evangelism in the 1990s, seeking for conversions to the faith. Further, he sought to establish a degree of discipline and conformity in the Church so that it could be seen to 'speak with one voice' on various issues. This new emphasis went against the Anglican grain in two ways: it threatened the carefully preserved tolerance of diversity typical of the liberal centre and it decreased the autonomy of the different provinces of the Anglican Communion, for example, in Africa and North America. Carey's insistence on a common voice echoes the managerialist message in private sector organisations to 'all sing from the same hymn sheet' (!), and the political requirement of New Labour MPs to 'stay on message'. To many, the 'voice' of the Anglicans under Carey carried rather strong evangelical overtones. Moreover, it was felt that Carey was risking the unity of the Church in seeking conformity at a point when the recently developed Synod, consisting of bishops, clergy and laity, rendered disagreement and debate highly public and contentious. The old days of keeping the wings of the Church attached by judicious backstage politicking seemed gone for ever. The stage was set for more conflict. The presenting issue was gay clergy and bishops, and the account of this continuing controversy which follows is based largely on the authoritative account of Stephen Bates.

Jeffrey, Gene and Rowan

The Anglican Church in England has adapted over the years to changes in the society which it serves. It has adapted to the realities of contraception, abortion, divorce and remarriage. In 1992 it finally agreed to ordain women as priests. The struggle to achieve this latter breakthrough was successful only after intense factional infighting, with the opposition defeated only because evangelicals were divided on the issue.[5] Some Anglo-Catholic clergy left to join the Roman Catholic Church, while others, mostly Anglo-Catholic, were bought off with a compromise. They could be ministered to by Provincial Episcopal Visitors, so-called 'flying bishops', who were not themselves in sympathy with the ordination of women.

This successful finessing of the issue was dangerous for two reasons. First, it blinded the moderate centre of the Church to the cost of the victory. The opposition had learned to organise, and was infuriated that the Church had appeared to bend to secular changes in society relating to women, rather than abiding by the word of Scripture or by Catholic tradition. And second, it had involved giving in to blackmail, in so far as those clergy who threatened to leave the Church altogether were given a potentially divisive sop in order to retain them. This had dangerous implications for the future. The benefits of institutional unity had perhaps been bought at too high a price.

The Sexual Offences Act of 1967 had long ago decriminalised homosexual activity between consenting adults in the UK. In 1976 the Lesbian and Gay Christian Movement (LGCM) had been formed to enable gay Christians to support each other and press for fuller acceptance within the Church. The Church had throughout its long history benefited from the services of gay clergy, with the LGCM estimating that some 20 per cent of clergy were gay,[6] well above the estimate for the population as a whole, with the Anglo-Catholic wing particularly likely to attract and welcome gays. The Church had traditionally turned a blind eye to the sexual orientation, and indeed to some extent to the sexual practice, of its clergy, provided that gays were discreet in style and not promiscuous in practice. However, this could not continue when the tabloid press, the conservative evangelicals and Peter Tatchell of OutRage, all for different reasons, were set on attacking, and in Tatchell's case, outing, gay clergy and bishops.

The church responded in its traditional way by commissioning a report to advise the bishops on the issue, but when it was presented in 1988 they refused to publish it. It was remarkably even-handed, and echoed earlier reports by the Quakers and the Methodists in distinguishing between different types of gay behaviour, for example, between promiscuous activity and committed partnerships. Implicit was the assumption that it was the quality of the relationship which was the real moral issue, not whether it was gay or straight.[7] Instead, the bishops published a document entitled *Issues in Human Sexuality* in 1991,[8] which was almost entirely concerned with gay relationships. It explicitly claimed not to be the last word on the topic, but its contents were sufficiently disappointing to gay hopes to persuade conservative evangelicals to claim it subsequently as Church doctrine written in stone. Archbishop Carey's desire to have the Church 'speak with one voice' may have encouraged this claim.

The report accepted that 'homophiles' (*sic*) fell short of the heterosexual ideal, but were equally loved and valued by God. Gay partnerships could be a blessing to the parties and to society at large, but sexual abstinence between gays was the ideal. In cases where the intention was a lifelong partnership, it was possible that the physical expression of the partners' affection for each other was acceptable. But it was not acceptable in the case of clergy, because of the distinctive nature of their vocation. This judgement was based on 'the insights which God had given the church through Scripture, tradition, and reasoned reflection on experience'. This reference was to the theological authority of the broad Church, not to Calvinist insistence on Scripture alone. Such 'reasoned reflection' unfortunately resulted in the obvious inconsistency of a position which allowed gay sex to the lay goose but not to the ordained gander; which permitted sex for straight but not for gay clergy; and which issued an open invitation to conservative evangelicals, the tabloid press and Peter Tatchell to engage in much prurient peeping through keyholes.

The Lambeth Conference is a meeting which occurs every ten years of all the bishops in the Anglican Communion worldwide. In 1998 it was due to concentrate on the urgent issue of Third World debt. However, it was hijacked by an apparently even more urgent issue: the ordination of gays. That issue itself was hijacked in a series of political manoeuvres which are explored in more detail below. The report *Issues in Human Sexuality* of 1991 was hardened up as a result of pressure largely from African bishops. A resolution was passed which rejected homosexual practice as incompatible with Scripture, and opposed the legitimising and blessing of same-sex unions and the ordination of those engaged in them. This resolution ('Lambeth 1.10'),[9] however, like the report, had an advisory status only. All such resolutions are subject to the autonomy of the different provinces of the Anglican Communion; British and Americans might moderate it in practice, Africans harden it up further. But in Archbishop Carey's context of 'speaking with one voice' it was greeted as a decisive victory by conservative evangelicals wherever they came from. Indeed, a Nigerian bishop appeared on prime time television seeking to exorcise the demon of homosexuality from Richard Kirker, the founder of LGCM.

Archbishop Rowan Williams succeeded Carey at the beginning of 2003, a liberal taking his turn after an evangelical, as was the custom. He had previously written in a liberal but typically academic tone about gays:

> In a church which accepts the legitimacy of contraception, the absolute condemnation of same-sex relations of intimacy must rely either on an abstract fundamentalist deployment of a number of very ambiguous texts or on a problematic and non-scriptural theory about natural complementarity, applied narrowly and crudely to physical differentiation without regard to psychological structures.[10]

He was therefore already suspected by evangelicals of failing to 'uphold the Church's agreed position on the issue'. However, in the country at large Williams' appointment was welcomed. He was only too clearly a more accomplished person than his predecessor, with a capacity for taking humane and humble symbolic actions, such as reviving the centuries-old custom of washing parishioners' feet on Maundy Thursday.

However, events were occurring in Canada which sounded a note of warning.[11] In 2003 an Anglican church in Vancouver blessed the gay union of two partners of 21 years. Canadian and American bishops had for some time been ordaining practising gay clergy. The blessing had not been the action of a rogue vicar: a long process of consultation in the diocese had culminated in a vote strongly in favour of permitting such blessings. On the other hand, the Reverend Margaret Marquardt permitted the exchange of rings, giving the blessing the aura of marriage. Archbishop Williams issued a statement expressing his sorrow, regretting that the diocese had gone further than the teaching of the Church or pastoral concern could justify, and that tension and division would inevitably result.

However, at the same time, much closer to home, Canon Jeffrey John was appointed Bishop of Reading by due process.[12] He was clearly the best candidate for the position in the view of Bishop Harries of Oxford, and the bishop's advisory committee consisting of two lay persons and two archdeacons. Both Archbishop Williams, Bishop Harries and the committee knew that John was gay, but was now celibate. John gave assurances that he would stay that way, and that he would support the Church's position as expressed in *Issues in Human Sexuality*. However, the evangelical press revealed the contents of a lecture by John to a private conference some five years before, in which he had referred to the Church colluding in a lie in respect of gay clergy. Evangelical opinion was mobilised fast, and 16 English bishops signed a letter urging the archbishop not to consecrate John. Archbishops from Africa and Australia intervened, threatening to split the Anglican Communion unless the appointment was rescinded. Williams, caught between a rock and a hard place, succumbed to this blackmail in order to maintain institutional unity. He required John to withdraw. Evangelicals subsequently issued statements praising John's integrity and sensitivity which, they said, had averted possible catastrophic consequences for the Church's unity.

But in 2004 a practising gay priest was consecrated as bishop in America.[13] In New Hampshire Gene Robinson was selected for consecration by due process, gaining a considerable majority of about two to one of the votes from each of the three electoral groups, bishops, clergy and laity. The American province of the Anglican Communion had exercised its autonomy. It is worth noting, however, that the Episcopal Church in America is one of the few denominations left in that country where liberal theological views are encouraged or even tolerated. Hence the same degree of evangelical opposition was not evidenced as in Jeffrey John's case, since American evangelicals have plenty of other places to go whereas liberals do not. English Anglicans are more 'inclusive'.

In a rush to minimise the damage he perceived likely to result from Bishop Robinson's appointment, Archbishop Williams summoned a crisis meeting of all the 38 Anglican archbishops, which occurred before Robinson's consecration service itself.[14] In the meantime, evangelicals said that the appointment was contrary to Scripture, and signalled their clear opposition. The American Church should be disciplined, they argued, or at the very least should be rebuked and called to repent. The Archbishops met and issued a statement, which said that many of the provinces of the Anglican Communion were likely to consider themselves out of communion with the Episcopal Church in America. However, the archbishop of that province, Frank Griswold, confirmed that the consecration would go ahead as planned. Archbishop Williams talked of crisis on the radio, and after the consecration 13 provinces announced themselves to be out of communion with the Episcopal Church in America. There was much talk among evangelicals of irrevocable divisions.

In traditional Anglican fashion, a commission was established under Robin Neames, Archbishop of Ireland, to examine not only the immediate causes of the crisis but also how the Church should best deal with grave issues of this type in the future. The implication was that somehow a disciplinary structure could be developed which would keep a unified framework across the Anglican Communion.

In October 2004 the commission reported.[15] It urged healing and reconciliation in place of harshness and rancour. It rejected any centralised power structure, such as the Curia of the Roman Catholic Church. Instead, the Archbishop of Canterbury should be aided by an advisory council, which would enhance his authority as 'first among equals'. All the provinces should agree a covenant, which would be obligatory and prevent provinces from going their own way. However, obligation was not taken to be synonymous with binding authority, nor was the covenant immutable. Parts of it could be developed and changed in the light of interpretation and practice.

In respect to the gay issue, the report criticised the Canadian and American Churches for failing to consider the impact of their decisions on the rest of the Communion. In particular, it rebuked those bishops who took part in Bishop Robinson's consecration service despite having been warned of the damaging consequences. It asked them to consider whether they should continue to serve on joint committees across the Communion, and whether Bishop Robinson, in particular, should attend any meetings of the Communion's bishops. It requested them to express regret for the hurt they had caused. It also urged a moratorium on the consecration of any more actively gay bishops. In an attempt to be even-handed, the report criticised the rancorous tone of the evangelical critics (e.g. the Dean of Sydney had likened Archbishop Williams to a theological prostitute, taking his salary under false pretences). It also condemned the divisive actions of bishops who had intervened to assist with pastoral oversight those parishes which voted against the consecration. In a final note of warning and despair, it concluded: 'There remains a very real danger that we will not choose to walk together. Should the call to halt and find ways of continuing in our present communion not be heeded, then we shall have to begin to learn to walk apart'.

It looks as though the traditional conciliatory skills of the Broad Church are finally failing, caught, not between Jeffrey, Gene and

Rowan, but rather between two irreconcilably different views of the nature and purpose of the Church in the world.

More recent events have confirmed this gloomy prognosis. In November 2005, nearly half of the world's archbishops rejected Williams' plea for dialogue, and urged him to 'rethink your personal view [on the gay issue] and embrace the church's consensus and to act on it, based as it is on the clear witness of Scripture'.[16] Their letter to him was available on evangelical websites around the world before he had opened it himself.

But why have things come to this apparent impasse? The bare bones of the story outlined above fail to indicate the global politics which now dominate the ecclesiastical stage. We need to dig deeper if we are to appreciate the sharpness of the conflict within the Anglican Communion.

Reform, mainstream and mission

What more theologically wholesome words could we possibly use to head this section: 'reform' indicating the need for constant renewal, 'mainstream' the need to avoid theological extremes and 'mission' the importance of facing outward rather than inward? In fact, all three are the titles, or part-titles, of pressure groups within the Anglican Church: Reform, Anglican Mainstream, and the Oxford Centre for Mission Studies. The activities of these and similar groups are indicative of the highly politicised nature of the Church today.

The current conflict within the Church is a conflict about values and about power.[17] The dispute about values drives the struggle for power. The two general tendencies, liberals and evangelicals, each wish to acquire and mobilise power to ensure that their value priorities determine what the Church does and says. A large moderate centre continues to be wary and tired of both, but it is the evangelicals, and to a lesser extent the liberals, who make all the political running.

The liberals wish to emphasise the inclusive nature of God's love and hence of the Church. The Church is for all, and has a particular duty to welcome minorities. Liberals do not regard secularism and modernity as counter to the faith, but seek to find evidence of God working within the secular world. They are more likely to be concerned to retain the institutional unity of the Church, since their high value on inclusivity necessarily includes even evangelicals. Evangelicals' values are very different. In the tradition of the original reformers, Calvin and Luther, they emphasise the authority of the Bible as the word of God, the necessity of personal conversion through the atoning death of Christ, and the importance of mission. Those who do not accept these doctrinal emphases are considered in error. Evangelicals wish to use power to ensure that the Church as a whole subscribes to these doctrines. Thus, while both parties wish to further their own values in practice, the liberals' preferred outcome would be inclusion, the evangelicals' conformity.

Politics can be defined as the acquisition and mobilisation of power to achieve one's aims without recourse to violence. Power may derive from a variety of sources, but essentially it has to be understood as a form of relationship between people.[18] In the case of liberals and evangelicals, the desired relationships are either of dominance or of tolerance. The evangelicals wish to exercise dominance over the Church as a whole in terms of imposing a uniformity of doctrine and practice, while the liberals wish to prevent them doing so by increasing its diversity. Over the last 20 years, the degree of politicisation of the Church has increased markedly, certainly relative to the previous century. The gay issue demonstrates extreme politicisation, with the result that the conflict has escalated to the point where institutional unity is threatened.

Historically, the Anglican moderate centre has used the power of its position as the national established Church very effectively. It has always insisted that it needs to steer a middle course in order to balance historically different views and contribute to national unity.[19] What is more, the Anglican Church as an institution owns the churches and the houses in which its clergy live and work, and contributes to their salaries. These two sources of position and resource power, respectively, represent a major asset. However, it has tended to take these sources of power for granted. It has been taken by surprise by the highly politicised acquisition and use of other sources of power by the evangelicals. Only special interest groups, such as the LGCM, have politicised to a similar degree on the liberal side, and only very recently has the liberal pressure group 'Inclusive Church' been established to contest its evangelical opponents.

So how have the evangelicals succeeded so well in making the running in the current conflict? What are the sources of their power, and how have they mobilised them? First, they have

numbers on their side. Evangelical churches are growing in proportion to others; 40 per cent of Anglican worshippers in Britain
are estimated to be on the evangelical wing, and 60 per cent of the
current clergy in training. More than a quarter of bishops are
evangelicals.[20] They were hugely reinforced in the 1980s by the
growth of the charismatic movement. Their frequently suburban
middle-class churches provide a lot of the income which an
increasingly impoverished Church needs. Threats by individual
churches or groups of churches to withhold this income from
diocesan funds have been used as a form of coercive power over
bishops of whom they do not approve.[21]

The numbers quoted, however, fail to do justice to the global
reach of the evangelicals' power base. They have assiduously
cultivated links with African and Asian bishops, who have proved
useful through the power of their votes in achieving political
objectives within the structures of the Church, especially, for
example, at Lambeth 1998. This numerical resource power is
balanced by *financial support* from the opposite geographical
direction: America. For example, the diocese of Dallas paid for
African bishops to go to a pre-Lambeth caucus meeting. At the
Conference itself, the wealthy American conservative, Howard
Ahmanson, funded the intense lobbying of the Oxford Centre for
Mission Studies.[22]

More important, the evangelicals have *political and organisational
support* from the Institute on Religion and Democracy, a lobbying
and pressure group operating from Washington DC. In the words
of *The New York Times*, this organisation 'is now playing a pivotal
role in the biggest battle over the future of American Protestantism
since churches split over slavery at the time of the Civil War'.[23] Its
aim is to enable fundamentalist control over the three remaining
large mainstream denominations in America, the United Methodist,
Episcopalian and Presbyterian churches. The Episcopalian church
is the self-governing American branch of the Anglican Communion.
The President of the Institute on Religion and Democracy, Diane
Knippers, heads up the Episcopal Action Directorate, aimed at
gaining control of that denomination. The *modus operandi* of the
Institute is to train up fundamentalist activists to take office and put
forward proposals at local, state and national levels of Church
governance. It supports the American Anglican Council, which
provides sympathetic oversight by conservative bishops for all those
who cannot agree with their own bishop. Knippers does not concern

herself only with the Episcopal Church in America, however, but attended the meeting of the Anglican archbishops in February 2005 when it was agreed that the Episcopal Church should withdraw from the Anglican Consultative Council, the executive body of the Anglican Communion.

The successful political use of power requires the mobilisation of the various resources available. Evangelicals have organised eagerly and effectively. The first thing they did was to select the right issue on which to fight. The gay issue was cleverly chosen to play to their own strengths and their opponents' weaknesses. Evangelicals could be persuaded to see the issue as a threat to their core beliefs. It appeared to be clearly and unambiguously addressed in the Bible (although in fact it is rarely and ambiguously referred to). Further, homosexuality can be construed as a series of sinful acts, and therefore something to be repented of. The gay person can be converted and receive the power of the Holy Spirit to help him or her to stop sinning. Even if it is agreed that homosexuality is a 'condition', or orientation, which the gay person did not choose, conversion involves a transformation through which the old self is cast aside in a process of rebirth.

The evangelicals' opponents' weakness was twofold. First, there were more gay clergy in the liberal camp, and especially in the Anglo-Catholic wing. Given the Church's published views on gays in *Issues in Human Sexuality*, gay clergy could be represented as disobeying the Church. Second, those who proselytised on behalf of gays did the liberals no favours. With friends like Peter Tatchell and Bishop Spong of Newark, New Jersey, who needed enemies? Indeed, the evangelicals used their media savvy to get Spong to say to the press that he believed the African bishops to be super-stitious.[24] By 1998 the evangelicals were absolutely clear that the gay issue was the line in the sand which they would draw and behind which they would fight. They had learned that they needed to be specific; an evangelical motion to the 1987 synod about sexual morality in general had been successfully finessed by the bishops.[25]

Of course, choosing the issue on which to fight gives more than mere tactical advantage. It enables the choosers to justify and legitimise their position, and to place it within their preferred framework of assumptions and meaning.[26] Having selected the issue and defined its context, they can dismiss anyone who steps outside that framework as irrelevant to the debate. Thus the general British public, and many Christians too, would want to say that the promotion of values such as justice, peace and compassion is what the Church should be concentrating on. They might refuse to argue the toss about the correct interpretation of the biblical passages about homosexuality, preferring instead to ask why the Bible should be treated as some sort of rule-book for the conduct of modern life. They might ask why the Church is so set on enforcing conformity when it is clear that there are different points of view. They might ask why the Church is concentrating on legalistic rulings about behaviour when its founders emphasised the 'fruits of the spirit' such as love, joy and peace. But all of these objections can be dismissed as irrelevant if the issue can be defined as one of Church doctrine and discipline. The ability to define the meaning of the conflict as well as its specific focus is a major source of power. Indeed, so is the ability to define the situation as one of conflict in defence of the truth rather than one of, say, challenge.

In order to mobilise all these different sources of power, *organisation* is crucial. American Protestants already had a history of successful use of modern political techniques when the fundamentalists took over the Southern Baptists in 1979. The lobbying prowess at the Lambeth Conference of the Oxford Centre for Mission Studies, funded from America, has already been noted. When the 'unsound liberal' Archbishop Williams was chosen (actually, he is relatively theologically conservative), such pressure groups as Reform and the Church Society organised a climate of open hostility to the appointment and to the person.[27] The archbishop was accused of being unsound on the gay issue and on the interpretation of the Bible in general. When he invited these conservative evangelicals to lunch to discuss the issues, one of their newspapers, *The English Churchman*, advised those attending: 'It is not enough to tell him that he should be silent about his views; it is not enough to tell him he shouldn't rock the boat . . . he must be told he is in error. He must be told he is a false shepherd of his sheep; he must repent his views'.[28]

However, it was the conflict regarding the consecration of Jeffrey John and Gene Robinson as bishops which really demonstrated the opportunistic organisational skills of the evangelicals. The Oxford Centre for Mission Studies succeeded in marshalling the support of Nigerian, Australian and West Indian bishops against the consecration of an English bishop. Evangelical English bishops mobilised themselves extremely quickly after the announcement of

John's appointment in order to write to Archbishop Williams in complaint. Clergy within the Oxford diocese were lobbied by phone to signal their opposition.[29] The text of an academic speech given by John some years before was dug out and sent to the press.[30]

In the case of Bishop Robinson, the evangelicals rapidly held caucus meetings of African and Asian evangelical archbishops who had been summoned by Rowan Williams to an emergency meeting. In a sophisticated press initiative, British evangelical bishops subtly implied that Robinson's liberal supporters were in fact being culturally insensitive in criticising the Africans.[31] As for the American Anglican Council, a conservative evangelical pressure group, it campaigned vigorously against Robinson's appointment. It threatened to set up an alternative traditional church, and it put in place a system of flying bishops to minister to those who disapproved of his consecration.[32]

The organisational and media sophistication of the evangelicals is evidenced in the title of their latest pressure group: 'Anglican Mainstream'. This is an eerie echo of the 1980s American moral majority, a stroke of marketing genius implying that most people in America were born-again Christians. The echo is probably not accidental. The influence of American evangelical Protestants worldwide is immense. It may well be the case that the links between evangelicals across denominations are stronger than those of different orientations within them. Many evangelicals may consider themselves to be worldwide evangelical Christians first, and Anglicans, Methodists or whatever, a long way behind second. The Anglican Communion may merely serve as a useful and comfortable base from which to spread their version of the Gospel.

The question is, will the Anglican Communion survive this determined takeover bid by the evangelicals? Will the real mainstream, the silent moderate centre, call their bluff when they threaten to leave (at the moment they cannot afford to)? Will it succeed in redefining the issues in its own terms rather than in theirs? Will it point out that it is *they* who are dividing the Church? Will it turn outwards and concentrate on serving its communities? To sum up, fittingly in the words of Stephen Bates:

> This has become in some ways an institution that is rather the reverse of the traditional bumbling, avuncular, wishy-washy Church of England. Just as the Militant Tendency tried to

subvert the old Labour Party in the 1980s, so the Church of England is being invaded by a Taliban Tendency with its own agenda and a strong determination to win. This is a takeover bid, to create a pure church of only one sort of believer. And it has found allies in the USA and the developing world.[33]

Or perhaps America has found allies in British evangelicals?

Evangelical fundamentalists?

What connection can the internal wranglings of the dear old Church of England possibly have with the destructive activities of Mohammed Atta? Surely it is grossly insulting to evangelical Christians to juxtapose the two case studies? I argue that the two cases are similar in that both constitute examples of fundamentalism. Both are characterised by same four of the five distinctive features of fundamentalism. There are many reasons why the first case resulted in a catastrophic assault while the second concerns merely a power struggle within the Church. But the underlying characteristics of a reactive religious movement are present in both. This certainly does not imply that conservative evangelical Anglicans are remotely likely to engage in violence to achieve their religious aims. It would be absolutely contrary to their beliefs and practice. However, abundant evidence of reactivity, dualism, authority and selectivity is only too clear in the above account of the gay issue.

Conservative evangelicals perceive themselves to be reacting against secular modernism. Like all fundamentalists, they see change in the secular world as generally for the worse. They feel that they are defending the true faith against these changes, which are not only corrupting the societies in which they live, but are also successfully subverting the Christian Church. The fact that they are out of step with the society they seek to serve only convinces them more firmly of the correctness of their own position. To quote a leading evangelical interviewed by Stephen Bates:

> There are puzzling questions about why God is allowing this. From time to time He exposes His people to severe trial. The Bible talks of pruning, purging, and so on, and the church always grows under persecution. If the church disintegrates, maybe that is because God discerns a better means for the

building of His Kingdom. God sometimes allows things to go in very strange directions.[34]

A letter signed by some evangelical bishops at the Lambeth Conference reads:

A crucial question is how we relate to the modern globalising culture which, although originating in the West, in one way or another powerfully impinges on us all . . .We must ask whether we are in danger of allowing this culture with its philosophical assumptions, economic system, sexual alternatives, and hidden idols to determine what we become.[35]

This form of reactivity tends to choose as its first opponent the liberals in the Church, the enemy within. To quote another prominent conservative evangelical:

The danger for the Christian church always comes from within, whether by persecution or apathy. It's false teaching which leads inevitably to false behaviour. You need sound doctrine and teaching to suit the congregation's itching ears . . . But we are moving into a world where the church is going to have to be counter-cultural, more so than it has been for a thousand years. But we are used to that; that is the challenge of Christian living. At the moment we are in danger of listening far more to the face of culture than to the Word of God.[36]

The second feature of fundamentalism, *dualism*, is also represented in the story of the gay issue in the Anglican Communion. The situation is construed by the conservative evangelicals as a conflict, a battle, a war, between two sides: us versus them, the faith versus the world, Scriptural truth versus apostate error, God versus the Devil, good versus evil, right versus wrong. The African bishops are said to have emerged from the Lambeth debate shouting 'Victory!'.[37] So careful are some evangelical vicars to defend the tender faith of their flock against the enemy that they sometimes require visiting preachers, including even the local bishop, to affirm that they abide by Lambeth 1:10. The Reverend David Banting says:

We would love to give people the benefit of the doubt, but the issue is Scripture. We want people here to be committed to the authority and essence of Scripture. If people are not governed by the word or speech of God or Lambeth 1:10, it would be difficult for us to welcome them here . . . There will be a realignment between those who believe in revelation and are seeking to live by it, and those basically who do not have time for the Bible and don't see it as part of God's revelation.[38]

Which leads us to the third defining feature of fundamentalism, the appeal to *authority* and in particular to that of the holy book. For evangelicals, this source of authority requires conformity to what the Bible plainly says. The Church only holds authority in so far as it faithfully maintains Scriptural doctrines. If it fails to do so, Scripture always wins out and the Church must be set right. The Bible is taken to be absolutely clear in its teachings. As the Reverend Banting somewhat condescendingly says, 'the Scripture is essentially clear. Even a ploughboy [*sic*] can understand it'.[39] It is interesting the way in which conservative evangelicals personify the Bible. They frequently say 'the Bible says', as though it is uttering God's word directly to us. The Bishop of Lewes even credits it with feelings: 'other ideas undermine God's idea of the family and are viewed by the Bible with disapproval'.[40] Typically of fundamentalists, the bishop considers that his views are those of the founders of the faith: 'There are reasons for holding the things that we have held for 2,000 years'. Yet he, and those like him, appear unable to understand that they are putting their own construction onto what a series of individuals from other cultures and from the pre-modern era wrote to specific readerships for particular purposes.

Finally, there is clear evidence of the fourth feature of fundamentalism, *selectivity*. For example, the evangelicals are very happy to extract a verse from the book of Leviticus which condemns 'man lying with mankind'. Most of them blanch, however, at applying the death penalty, which the verse also mandates. They also hesitate about forbidding pork, rabbit, shellfish and tattoos, all forbidden in the Jewish code of Leviticus. They are selective in another way also. They choose a topic, homosexuality, which is very seldom mentioned in the Bible. The importance of love, equity and commitment in relationships is, however, a frequent theme. Why is this not selected as an issue of importance? The answer, of course, is that it is not an issue which can be used to divide the Church.

Chapter 6

Social identity, Atta and the Anglicans

Conflict

I now seek to apply SID to the case studies of the previous two chapters. Clearly, this application is *post hoc* rather than predictive, and thus meets few of the criteria for the testing of hypotheses, either in the laboratory or in a field experiment. Nevertheless, the exercise has value since it puts some flesh and bones onto the rather dry theory and evidence that characterise the academic literature. At least we may determine whether SID gives a convincing social psychological account of fundamentalisms as they happen on the ground. We know that underlying the immense variety of fundamentalisms are five distinctive features. Why are ordinary people attracted to these features, and why do they believe and act as they do?

The most basic characteristic of fundamentalists is that *they believe that they are involved in a conflict*. They are struggling for their survival against modernism. The evangelical Anglicans (Chapter 5) are battling for control of their denomination, in order to ward off the secular liberal threat to the truth. Osama bin Laden (Chapter 4) is fighting in what he believes to be a cosmic conflict between Allah and His enemies. Thus we would expect all of the conditions which SID requires for the occurrence of in-group versus out-group conflict to be met in these cases.

To recapitulate (see pp. 30–35), these conditions are, first, that the in-group social identity should be strongly internalised; second, that it should be possible for in-group members to compare and contrast themselves with other groups; and third, that the out-group has to be relevant to the in-group's survival and success. In both the case studies, these three conditions are met.

First, we consider the *group comparison* condition: for conflict to occur, comparisons with the out-group must be possible. How clearly did the Anglican evangelicals and bin Laden's followers distinguish themselves from their chosen out-group? More specifically, how did they achieve a tight and homogeneous prototype? How did they select and stereotype their enemy? And how did they maximise the differences between prototype and stereotype (see pp. 32–33)?

The Anglican evangelicals were fairly clear who was their enemy. Like the first fundamentalists, the American Protestants of the 1920s, their out-group was the apostate Church. It has, in their view, been seduced into error in its doctrine and practice by the secular society of its times. Indeed, an evangelical spokesman argued that secularism is the real enemy (see p. 92). There is therefore some ambiguity as to the inclusiveness of the out-group: liberal Anglicans, or secularism. The selection of the apostate Church as the immediate out-group has major consequences for the composition of the *prototype*. By way of contrast to the apostate liberals, the prototypical evangelical is above all sound in doctrine and practice. To believe and affirm correct doctrine, and to abide by the rules of conduct and practice which derive from it, are the key features of the evangelical prototype. Indeed, it is such an important element that the Rev. David Banting insists on all visiting preachers affirming their acceptance of heterosexual orthodoxy (see p. 93). Otherwise they might, after all, lead his flock astray on this fundamentally important doctrinal matter. The prototype would be at risk, and the distinctiveness from the out-group would be compromised.

For the hijackers, too, there was a close relationship between the nature of the out-group and the contents of their own prototype. Their out-group was the overbearing and arrogant secular world, personified by the Great Satan, America. This out-group was, in secular terms, a powerful and hostile foe, bent upon the destruction of the true faith. Therefore, the prototypical features were those of the good soldier of Allah: faithful and steadfast to the end, using the sacred weapons of prayer and purity to overcome the powerful secular enemy. Mohammed Atta's instructions continually reinforce these prototypical elements.

In both cases, *depersonalisation* is clearly evident. Evangelicals insist that certain religious steps must be experienced by each and every born-again Christian. Among these is a conversion experience, followed by assent to, and practice of, Evangelical BVNs.[1] Behaviour which violates these BVNs is disapproved; for example, a social and personal identity as gay is unacceptable. Doctrinal orthodoxy may be the paramount feature in the proto-type, but it is used to inform attitudes about moral issues and behavioural conformity, and hence secures a highly consistent and distinctive prototype. There is limited room for personal identity and diversity. Atta's reinforcement of the hijackers' prototype as militant Muslims includes no hints of personal identities what-soever. Each of Allah's warriors is interchangeable in the struggle against the infidel.

The same depersonalisation is evident in the *stereotypes* of the out-group held by evangelicals and hijackers alike. For example, Atta emphasises that the hijackers are not to treat the passengers as individual enemies. They are not to show personal animosity towards them, but rather treat them all simply as representatives of the enemy.[2] Such depersonalisation obviously enables the hijackers to avoid applying any other category to their victims, for example, parent or spouse. In his attempt to exorcise Rev. Richard Kirker of his 'demon of homosexuality', the evangelical Bishop Chukwuma of Nigeria said, 'We have overcome carnality, just as the light will overcome darkness'.[3] Kirker was, for the bishop, no more than a representative of the enemy, 'carnality' or 'darkness'.

The stereotypes of the out-group used by the evangelicals and the hijackers clearly serve to reinforce the distinctiveness of the in-group, and the difference between in-group and out-group. The relatively few elements of the stereotype which are evidenced in the two cases exemplify this function. For evangelicals, liberal clergy are unsound heretics who are failing their flocks and have an agenda of subverting orthodoxy. As far as Mohammed Atta is concerned, the enemy are infidels and idolators who deny God and break his laws (the opposite of the prototypical faithful soldier).

SID suggests (see p. 34) that when an out-group is particularly varied and inclusive, the prototype of the in-group and its leadership is likely to be more extreme, in order to maintain the in-group's distinctiveness. The out-group for Mohammed Atta is the whole of the rest of the world. The prototype, and the leadership which it generates, is consequently extreme. For the evangelicals, the out-group is the apostate Church, a much less inclusive category. Thus the prototype relates primarily to doctrine, and the leadership is careful to appear simply to be upholding accepted orthodoxy. We are mainstream, they imply; it is the liberals who are the dissident minority.[4]

Finally, SID asserts that the perception of the *social context* is a crucial determinant of the degree of distinctiveness between the parties, and hence of the severity of the conflict. Atta perceived the context as one in which an all-consuming cosmic war between Allah and His enemies is in progress. The distinction between the soldiers of Allah and the infidel followers of the Great Satan could not be clearer, and the conflict could not be, literally, bloodier. The evangelical Anglicans, on the other hand, see the context as primarily theological. Theirs is the pure view of doctrinal orthodoxy, whereas their opponents are seduced by the sirens of secularism.

The choice of issue by the evangelicals on which to draw their line in the sand beyond which they will not go is, however, highly significant. For it places the conflict in the arena of sexual morality, in America a prominent political issue. The context for the evangelicals is therefore also one of conflict between religious orthodoxy and secular laxity and relativism. The social, economic and political circumstances of the two in-groups are extremely different. However, the out-group for them both may ultimately be the secular world, personified in one case as liberal Anglicans and in the other as the Great Satan. The difference is that evangelicals conduct their struggle with politics and persuasion; Atta and his like with bombs and terror.

Another condition which SID proposes as necessary for group conflict to occur is that the social identity of the in-group is *strongly internalised into the self*. If a social identity is going to take a dominant role in directing behaviour, then it has to be central to the self, and habitually salient in the mind of the group member. In a wide variety of situations, the member has to construe him or herself in terms of this central identity, but especially whenever it is possible to construe others as an out-group.

The centrality of their identity as militant Muslims cannot be in doubt for the hijackers. They volunteered to fight for the cause in Chechnya before being redirected towards the twin towers, thus indicating the all-consuming nature of their social identity. Other potential identities, for example that of husband and father, were subordinated to their religion. Atta is reported to have been attracted to a woman, but to have rejected her on the grounds that she was too assertive (in other words, not sufficiently prototypical).[5]

The language and concepts of Atta's instructions to the hijackers are totally suffused with the BVNs of his group. Only if those BVNs had been internalised as the central element of their selves could the hijackers have understood and acted upon them. It took considerable work by scholars to tease out all the religious allusions and meanings in the document.[6]

Evangelicals, too, have their own language. It explicitly includes within, and excludes from, the in-group. The distinctions made are those between the sound and the unsound; the biblical and the unbiblical; orthodoxy and heresy; the pure and simple versus the ambiguous and compromised. The language represents a clear and simple set of BVNs which are internally logically consistent, and which apply to behaviour in a wide range of contexts.

The lives of Anglican evangelicals are bound up very strongly in their local congregations, where their social identity as evangelicals is reinforced, for their leaders ensure that evangelical BVNs are dominant. This may even be true of the extraordinarily successful Alpha study course, which welcomes open enquiry, but whose authors apparently hold to some very specific positions on moral issues.[7] We cannot really judge how central to their selves is the evangelical identity for the ordinary Anglican member, however. Research on American evangelicals suggests that their attitudes are a lot more nuanced than one might expect,[8] probably because they have other strong social identities besides that of born-again believer. We can, however, be clear about the centrality of the evangelical identity for evangelical leaders. It is they who are making the political running in the battle for power in their denomination, a battle which appears to occupy considerably more of their time and attention than their other priestly tasks.

The final condition to be fulfilled if social identities are to result in conflict is that the perceived out-group has to be *relevant* for the in-group. First, according to SID, the out-group may present a perceived threat to the *security* of the in-group. The threat for the hijackers was one of life and death. Their Muslim identity was, they felt, under threat of annihilation by the secular world, although they believed Allah would gain the ultimate victory. And, because of the specific group to which they belonged, their lives were literally under threat from infidels. As for the evangelicals, what is threatened is the authority and purity of doctrine. To the extent that their prototype is one of obedience to pure biblical doctrine, any out-group, in particular Anglican liberals, which threatens doctrine by its disobedience is a threat to their prototype, and therefore to their selves.

Hence for both parties, the preferred out-group is a threat to their identity. However, a second aspect of relevance, SID suggests, is the *permeability* of the social categories. How easy is it for ideas or people from outside the group to enter and change its BVNs? The right to challenge existing BVNs for both our case-study groups is hard won by leaders who have served their time and gained their idiosyncracy credit (see p. 33) as a result. Sayyid Qutb had languished in prison, for example. The groups and their BVNs are otherwise relatively impermeable to the outside world. Other ideas are, to any absolutist, by definition wrong. The prototype is kept as secure and distinct as possible.

Thus for both Atta and the Anglicans, the situation as they construe it is one of threat to a beleaguered fortress: the fortress of the faithful Muslim world for Atta, and that of pure biblical doctrine for the Anglicans. The combination of insecurity and impermeability is certain to result in conflict.

Thus all the conditions for conflict cited by SID are clearly met in our case studies. There is ample opportunity for comparison between in-group and out-group; the social identities of the two in-groups are central to their selves; and the perceived out-groups are highly relevant for the in-groups. The case studies support the contention that SID offers a good explanation for the struggle and conflict to which these two contemporary examples of fundament-alism devote themselves. Now, we must ask, does SID account equally satisfactorily for individuals' motivation to be involved in fundamentalisms in the first place?

Motivation

SID is very successful at explaining why people are motivated to join and stay with groups. This is because of the way in which the social identity gained from belonging is internalised and incor-porated into the self. Hence, what happens to the group affects the self. If the group is victorious, one gains *self-esteem* because it is the self that is victorious by proxy. If the group is threatened, the self is threatened, and the need to preserve it is equally important. Therefore the tendency of all fundamentalisms to see themselves as at threat, and in a struggle for survival and victory, makes moti-vation relating to the self much more likely to occur.

This is clearly evidenced in the cases of the hijackers and of the evangelicals. The hijackers were motivated by the prospect of a great victory. They would be Allah's victorious shock-troops, destined for a famous martyrdom. Allah would be vindicated over the Great Satan, and his faithful servants the world over would gain pride in Islam and reject the arrogant insults of the infidels. As for the evangelicals, we have already noted their triumphalism as they succeeded in winning a few political battles within the Church: 'An amazing thing has happened', says the Evangelical Bishop of Lewes, 'Over the last fifty years, we have grown phenomenally'.[9] But fear of defeat is just as motivating as prospects of victory, for the survival of the self is as important as the growth of self-esteem.

The very fact of belonging can increase self-esteem, because it requires a degree of acceptance by one's fellow adherents. But as soon as the adherent internalises a distinctive social identity with a clear prototype, and an equally definite stereotype of the out-group, self-esteem blossoms for all sorts of other reasons. First, the prototype and its associated BVNs are strongly approved of by fellow adherents. By this approval they are also approving of the individual member's self, since the prototype is now internalised. Such approval is a far greater boost to self-esteem than mere acceptance into the group. Atta's instructions explicitly praise the prototype of the faithful and enduring soldier of Allah: 'You must remember to make supplications wherever you go, and any time you do anything, and God is with his faithful servants. He will protect them and make their tasks easier, and give them success and control and victory and everything . . .'.[10]

A second boost to self-esteem is derived from the actual content of the BVNs themselves. Adherents are assured that they are actually very worthy people. Evangelicals have accepted God's free gift of salvation and are saved for evermore. The hijackers are told: 'This test from almighty God is to raise your level and erase your sins . . . Almighty God said: "Did you think you could go to heaven before God knows whom amongst you have fought for him and are patient?"'.[11] The 'level' to which Atta refers is the higher level in heaven that the hijackers will reach as a consequence of their actions.

Self-esteem is also enhanced by the comparison of one's own prototype with the stereotype of the out-group. Since the stereotype often consists of elements which are the bad opposites of the good prototypical features, looking and feeling good about oneself is not difficult. 'If the Liberals are starting from their own experience', says the Rev. Banting, 'they are making God in their own image. The danger for the Christian church always comes from within, whether by persecution or apathy. It's false teaching which leads inevitably to false behaviour. You need sound doctrine and teaching to suit the congregation's itching ears'.[12]

Or, from the Rev. Sandy Millar, vicar of Holy Trinity, Brompton: 'I am not attacking anybody, because we're not fighting flesh and blood, but a new demonic ideology that is attacking the very fabric of the church'.[13] It certainly boosts the self-esteem to be compared by implication with those who teach falsely, behave falsely and are in thrall to a demonic ideology. As for the hijackers, their virtue as faithful soldiers of Allah is pointed up by Atta's references to their victims. They are 'the allies of Satan, who are the brothers of the Devil'. This certainly implies that we, in contrast, are 'the allies of God, who are the brothers of Allah'. So important is the motivating power of self-esteem that it is possible to argue that all extremist social groups depend on offering a central social identity for people who lack one.[14]

The second major motivation for belonging to a group and internalising a social identity is the consequent *reduction of uncertainty*. Perhaps the most basic form of uncertainty is uncertainty about the self. 'Who am I?' is the existential dilemma, especially if one's family and cultural roots have recently been disturbed in the process of industrialisation. Clearly, a reduction of existential uncertainty is likely to boost one's self-esteem. It is very hard to value oneself positively if one does not know who one is.

Fundamentalisms provide their adherents with a clear account of who they are. At the cosmic level, they are assured that they have a particular role in world history. In the case of the hijackers, they are striking a blow for God in the struggle with evil, and their reward is a place in the gallery of martyrs. The Anglican evangelicals are upholding the great tradition of the Reformation, maintaining God's truth in the face of corrupt secular assaults. Any movement which sees itself primarily as fighting a war offers its troops a clear role as defenders of the faith.

However, the cosmic level of meaning is rarely enough for the less ideologically rarefied adherents. The BVNs of the fundamentalism provide a far more grounded and detailed set of meanings. Their belief system provides them with an internally consistent and authoritative account of what they should believe about themselves, about others, about the world and about God.

In the case of the evangelical Anglicans, the authority for their BVNs comes directly from the Bible. Their own construction of 'what the Bible says' gives a clear and simple theology, in starkly binary terms. The individual is either saved or unsaved, and they are only saved through acceptance of the once-for-all atoning sacrifice of Christ on the Cross. They are then secure for a blessed eternity. As Billy Graham's soloist, George Beverly Shea, used to sing:

> Blessed assurance, Jesus is mine:
> O what a foretaste of glory divine!
> Heir of salvation, purchase of God;
> Born of His Spirit, washed in His blood.[15]

Of course, evangelical theology is, for its professionals and devotees, as complex as any other theology. But its fundamentals are simple propositions which are easy to comprehend and act on, once one accepts various assumptions. Central among these is that the Bible is the word of God speaking directly to the individual. Hence it provides the basis not only for theological belief, but also for values and norms of behaviour. In the struggle over gay priests and bishops, the social rules which may or may not have governed the lives of the Jews[16] or of the early Corinthian Christians[17] are cited as reasons why priests and bishops must not be gay.

The direct translation to modern practice is not made quite so easily, however. Individuals reading the Bible for themselves, and making evangelical assumptions about the nature of its authority, may sometimes find themselves facing a dilemma. Which of the values and norms of behaviour described and prescribed in the Bible should they believe for themselves and act upon? Should they, for example, eat shellfish (prohibited to the Jews as recorded in the book of Leviticus)? Here, however, orthodoxy and its zealous defenders, such as the Rev. Banting, are only too willing to make it clear what is and what is not required of the believer. Hence evangelicals enjoy an enviable certainty about what to believe, what values to prioritise and what norms of behaviour to follow. Their fundamentalist membership reduces, if not elim-inates, any uncertainty about who they are, and about their place in the material and spiritual world.

Atta's message to the hijackers echoes a similar certainty, but of course was not written as a considered statement of BVNs. When we turn to the writings of his theological heroes, Mawdudi and Qutb, however, coherent accounts of a stark and simple belief system, and its implications for values and behaviour, become evident. 'Islam wants and requires the entire inhabited world', states Mawdudi (see p. 66). Hence Muslims should engage in a revolutionary *jihad* in order to achieve this prize. And Qutb argues (see p. 68) that all forms of government other than a strict Muslim theocracy are forms of slavery. All human societies are *jahili*, the enemy. Hence every human value or social behaviour which is not sanctioned in Sharia law is to be condemned.

There is one more psychological benefit which fundamentalist certainty brings. Fundamentalists have, in the form of stereotypes, clear and simple views of other groups. They believe that they know the sort of people their enemies are, and therefore the sort of action they are likely to take. This enables them to plan ahead and feel that they are in control of outcomes. To have this confidence increases their certainty about what will happen in the future; it also enhances their self-esteem as people with power and control.

Thus the Bishop of Lewes knows very well what sort of people liberals are: 'I think some Liberals are trying it on', he opines, 'I think there is a calculated movement in some quarters. It is the radical liberal agenda that is always plotting. It is Machiavellian'.[18] The perception of their Machiavellian plotting means, of course, that we have to be even more wise and cunning ourselves in order to overcome it. The politics of the Lambeth Conference were brilliantly managed by the evangelicals. But they needed the justification which the perception of plotting by the liberals provides: 'We do our worst when we are plotting', the bishop admits, and then brings in divine authority for further support: 'Jesus does say be as wise as serpents' (note his use of the present tense). Having plotted more effectively than the enemy, they could feel satisfied with their control over the outcome: 'Victory', shouted the African bishops exultantly.

Sayyid Qutb offers his own clear programme for action on the basis of a similar conspiracy stereotype:

> *Jahiliyaah* [the enemy] always takes the form of a living movement in a society and has its own leadership, its own concepts and values, and its own traditions, habits and feelings. It is an

organised society, and there is a close cooperation and loyalty among its individuals, and it is always ready and alive to defend its existence consciously or unconsciously. It crushes all elements that seem to be dangerous to its personality. When *jahiliyaah* takes the form not of a 'theory' but of an active movement in this fashion, then any attempt to abolish it and to bring people back to Allah would be useless if it presented Islam merely as a theory. Since *jahiliyaah* controls the practical world and has a living and active organisation for its support, mere theoretical efforts to fight it cannot even be equal to it, much less superior. When the purpose is to abolish the existing system and to replace it with a new system [radical Islam] which in its characteristic principles and all its general and particular aspects, is different from the controlling *jahili* system, then it stands to reason that this new system should also come into the battlefield as an organised movement and a viable group. It should come into the battlefield with a determination that its strategy, its social organisation, and the relationship between its individuals should be firmer and more powerful than the existing *jahili* system.[19]

This wordy stereotype of the foe as systematically organised to conquer enables the writer to advocate the use of the same methods. The bishop sought to overcome perceived plotting with more effective plotting; the Islamist matched perceived power with greater power. Both felt that they had trumped their opponent, and so were in control of outcomes.

So SID provides a clear theoretical account of how the needs for self-esteem and for uncertainty reduction drive loyalty to the two fundamentalisms of our case studies. However, it also helps us to understand how the social identity which meets these needs is itself derived from the conflict between fundamentalisms and their out-groups.

Conflict, identity and motivation

SID proposes that the keener the conflict, the more central and important the in-group social identity will become. This is because, in conflict situations, greater efforts will be made to distinguish one's own group from the out-group. The various ways of high-lighting the distinctiveness of the in-group include the firming up of prototype and stereotype, and increased depersonalisation of both groups. Furthermore, the in-group social identity will be more salient in social situations. Hence, any social situation is more likely to be construed as one of in-group versus out-group conflict.

SID also indicates that the more inclusive the out-group, the more extreme the in-group prototype and leadership become. They have to be extreme in order to clearly distinguish the in-group from the hugely varied out-group. Moreover, if the out-group is so inclusive as to constitute the whole of the rest of the world (as it does in the case of militant Islam), then there are no other social identities available to internalise into the self. Thus the keener the conflict and the more general the enemy, the more central the social identity becomes, to the point where it is the only social identity which the individual possesses.

The difference between the Anglicans and the hijackers in the centrality and salience of their respective social identities illustrates these theoretical propositions. Evangelical Anglicans are likely to have several other relatively salient and central social identities than their evangelical identity, for example, parent, spouse/partner, occupation, nationality and so on. As noted above, American evidence indicates that ordinary evangelicals' attitudes on social/ moral issues are not nearly as clear cut as the pronouncements of their leaders would suggest.[20] One reason for this might be that their social identity as, for example, spouse, leads them to recognise that many evangelicals divorce, and therefore that the clear black and white evangelical BVNs need some softening to accord with the reality of their lives. It is noteworthy that nearly all the running in the Anglican conflict is being made by the clergy, whose vocation to defend the faith is part of their ordained evangelical identity. Rev. Banting is very concerned that his 'sheep' (his congregation) should not be led astray. They, by implication, are much less secure in their doctrinal soundness than he is. The power of evangelical leaders over the evangelical agenda is enhanced by their ability to represent their BVNs as given directly by God through the Bible. But for lay Anglicans, other social identities are likely to render the evangelical identity less central, salient and extreme than it appears to be for their ordained leaders.

No such moderating social identities soften the extreme BVNs of the hijackers, however. The entire rest of the world, including their own nation and the vast majority of their fellow Muslims, are their out-group. There is no social identity available to them other than that of Muslim revolutionary. They cannot even embrace their traditional religion: according to Qutb:

> all the existing so-called 'Muslim' societies are also *jahili* societies. We classify them among *jahili* societies not because they believe in other deities besides God, nor because they worship anyone other than God, but because their way of life is not based on submission to God alone. Although they believe in the unity of God, still they have relegated the legislative attribute of God to others, and submit to this authority, and from this authority they derive their systems, their traditions and customs, their laws, their values and standards, and almost every practice of life.[21]

Moreover, the hijackers' social identity as the vanguard of the Muslim revolution gave them an immense feeling of spiritual and moral superiority (see p. 7). Depersonalised by their prototype, and desocialised by the absence of any other possible social identities, the hijackers were ideal martyr material for their leaders. What little we know of Atta's life suggests that, by 2001, he had rejected any other social identities that were open to him. He had given up the idea of marriage and his duties as son were subjugated to his revolutionary zeal.

Thus the central feature of fundamentalisms, their struggle against secularism, underpins the application of SID in the attempt to understand them from a psychological perspective. For it is the starkness of the distinction between the in-group and the out-group which results in extreme social identities. These include prototypes of the fundamentalist groups and stereotypes of their enemies which are the reverse image of each other. Fundamentalisms depend totally on the existence of their enemy. The enemy may be almost entirely a construction of their own imagination: the stereotype may be derived directly from the prototype. Hence the power of the fundamentalist leaders to determine prototypes and their associated stereotypes is crucial, for without an enemy the movement has no reason to exist, and they lose their power. When their enemy defines them in turn as *their* enemy, fundamentalist leaders are overjoyed. George W. Bush did bin Laden's work for him.

However, the prototype and its associated BVNs are not only vital for maintaining the momentum of the struggle. They also, according to SID, provide the motivating power for action by adherents. If the most powerful human motives relate to the security, maintenance and enhancement of the self, then the social identity of fundamentalist adherents provides extraordinarily powerful motivation. The astonishment of non-fundamentalists that some fundamentalists are willing to go to a certain death for their cause suggests the unique nature of this power. By means of its account of how social identities are internalised into the self, SID makes the crucial theoretical link between the social struggle and the individual motivation.

The two case studies concern two apparently totally different groups of people. One group has profoundly changed world politics by its violent activities. The other, with its obscure theological arguments, has barely impinged upon secular consciousness. The one is spawned by a set of social, political and economic factors which do not apply to the other. The one is generally condemned for its terrorism; the other is very often recognised for its service to the community. Yet the two resemble each other in this one way: both are examples of fundamentalisms, fulfilling at least four of the five defining criteria for inclusion into that category.

We may lose sight of this commonality if we concentrate on the issue of why the one turned so easily to violent action while the other would not dream of doing so.[22,23] This is indeed a profoundly important question which psychologists will need to address urgently. The ultimately more important issue, however, is to understand why people belong to fundamentalist movements in the first place. SID provides a psychological explanation, which can at present only be considered promising. The piecemeal nature of the evidence assembled in Chapter 3, and the *post hoc* nature of the case studies cannot constitute real empirical support as yet.

However, there is nothing so practical as a good theory. If SID provides a good explanation, it should be possible to derive predictions from the theory regarding potential ways of reducing damaging conflict resulting from fundamentalisms. The last chapter is devoted to an attempt to do so.

Chapter 7

The management of fundamentalist conflicts

Resolution, management or victory?

We may *understand* fundamentalism better by applying SID to the existing research literature (Chapter 3) and to two very different case studies (Chapters 4 and 5). But what help does the theory give us in our efforts to *actively deal* with such conflicts as those in which Anglicans and al-Qaeda are engaged? It is obvious that these two cases are different in very many respects, the most important being that one is a struggle for power within a Christian denomination, while the other is a violent assault on the symbols of global secular power. Yet it has proved possible to analyse both cases satisfactorily in terms of SID, so there are perhaps some general pointers to managing fundamentalist conflicts which may be derived from the theory. I will explore them in this chapter.

First, however, we must establish why fundamentalist conflict needs to be addressed. It is often argued that conflict does not necessarily have bad outcomes for one or both parties. Frequently, it results in a new synthesis which is better adapted to the needs of the parties. So, for example, it is possible that a synthesis of evangelical and liberal theology might benefit both parties in the Anglican conflict by making the Church more attractive to outsiders and more capable of having an effective impact in the world. Such a successful *resolution* of conflict, however, cannot occur unless a number of demanding conditions are met.[1]

First, the parties have to analyse the conflict situation, usually with the help of a third party. This is likely to require the recognition that the other has both substantive and subjective issues which both parties must address.[2] Next, the stereotypes that each holds of the other, and their perceptions of the relationship, are two subjective elements which must be moderated before a climate conducive to addressing the substantive issues can be achieved. Arriving at a successful solution depends on the parties understanding their own and the others' motivations, aspirations and constraints. However, even this greater understanding of the other is not in itself sufficient to guarantee a solution. The substantive issues must also be confronted:

> Recognition of and respect among distinct identity groups in cultural and political terms must go hand in hand with equality of opportunity in economic [or any other] terms. Conflict resolution thus does not imply assimilation or homogenisation, although members of distinct identity groups may share a political or national identity as well; but it does imply a mosaic of integrated social groups, cooperating independently for mutual benefit.[3]

Clearly, the conditions for successful conflict resolution are demanding. 'Resolution' implies that the new relationship between the parties can be sustained in the future so that they will never again resort to conflict as a way of settling their differences. It is immediately evident that these conditions are absent from the two conflicts which we have analysed in depth. Engaging in meaningful dialogue in which each party shows the other respect appears to be a bridge too far for the Anglicans, and a whole world too far for al-Qaeda. In both cases, the conflict has escalated to a point where respect and dialogue are out of the question. Threats and counter-threats, actions and reactions, have fed upon each other in a positive feedback loop. Each party acts towards the other in a way which is guaranteed to justify their initial mistrust, because it provokes a hostile reaction.[4] For example, evangelical and liberal Anglicans perceive each other as Machiavellian plotters, and so act in ways which ensure that these stereotypes are accurate (see p. 103). Actions are based upon prototypes of the in-group and stereotypes of the out-group, and the parties are becoming more and more intransigent. When conflicts have escalated this far, there appears to be little hope of resolution and favourable outcomes, although we should note that Anglican beliefs allow for the possibility of reconciliation through the grace of God, however hopeless the situation appears.

Not only have fundamentalist conflicts, including our two case studies, usually escalated beyond the possible realisation of the necessary conditions for conflict resolution, they are also a particularly difficult type of conflict to resolve. They are conflicts of ideology, relating to beliefs and values which are incompatible, rather than conflicts of interest which might be amenable to a win-win solution, or at the worst, to an equitable division of the limited cake. Certain conflicts of interest might nevertheless also be present. For example, it may not be in the interests of western nations for Arab nations to be ruled by Islamic theocracies. However, these possible conflicts of interest are subordinate to the ideological battle. It is social identities, and therefore selves, which are primarily at stake.

Thus conflict resolution is not a realistic objective. There remain two alternative possible aims: *conflict carried through to a conclusion* or *conflict management or mitigation*.[5] Both parties in both case studies appear to have opted for the former alternative. Evangelical Anglicans have for some time aimed for victory (control of the denomination). The liberals seem to have begun to resolve the age-old liberal dilemma by judging that tolerating the intolerant is too much of a one-way street.[6] Al-Qaeda's *raison d'être* is violent conflict, and much of the rest of the world has rapidly assumed the role of enemy. It is extremely easy for modern secular people to treat fundamentalists as 'them', an out-group of deluded aliens, but in so doing we are fulfilling their need to be the persecuted but faithful few, and thereby fuelling the conflict. The outcome of victory for one party is, of course, the temporary defeat of the other, but also the possible development of a yet more extreme reactionary movement. The only alternative appears to be to adopt another iconic product of modernity: *management*. What general directions for the successful management of fundamentalist conflict does SID have to offer?

Opportunities for comparison

We have already noted that SID does not imply that members of a social category are automatically hostile to members of other categories. Three main conditions have to be met before conflict ensues. To recapitulate, these are as follows: first, there has to be opportunity for social comparison of one's own group with out-group(s); second, there has to be a context which gives rise to insecurity and impermeability of the in-group; and third, the in-group identity has to be centrally important to the self. The practical implication of SID is obviously that if we can remove or mitigate these conditions, then we can decrease the degree of conflict and make it more manageable. First, then, how can we decrease the opportunity for social comparisons and change the categories with which comparisons are made?

It is important to remember that, according to SID, social categories can exist merely in the mind; they do not necessarily have to be constituted by face-to-face groups, or even by virtual groups: 'A group [exists] psychologically when people share a collective self-definition'.[7] Usually, face-to-face groups constitute sub-identities nested within the superordinate social identity. So, for example, members of All Souls Church, Langham Place, London, are a face-to-face group constituting a nested identity within the category 'evangelical Christian'. The group of hijackers were a sub-set of militant Islam.

Throughout the case studies, it was evident that fundamentalist ideologies are at their most powerful and destructive when they can clearly differentiate themselves from huge inclusive abstract categories. Atta and his colleagues considered all those other than militant Islamists such as themselves as *jahili*. Anglican evangelicals waver between identifying their opponents as Anglican liberals, or secularism. In order to manage the social comparison process, then, it will be necessary to reduce the opportunity to make such comparisons, and to change the out-group with whom the comparison is made.

First, however, we need to recapitulate why it is that social comparisons are so important. Social comparisons with other groups enable members to differentiate their own social identity clearly. The more clear and distinct their identity, the less uncertainty they feel about themselves. Furthermore, the greater their distinctiveness from the other, the greater, potentially, is their self-esteem by way of comparison. From the social comparison process is derived the cognitive condition for conflict: depersonalisation in the form of prototypes and stereotypes. To reduce the opportunity for comparison, therefore, makes it more difficult to establish depersonalisation. Prototypes and stereotypes become softer and more complex.

How might opportunity for comparison be reduced? One obvious and not entirely facetious strategy is to make it absolutely clear to the fundamentalist group in question that it is welcome to *withdraw from the modern world*, and that its right to do so is guaranteed (provided that it abides by the law). The Amesh are one example of such withdrawal. No regular social comparisons are then possible for them, or for us. However, this solution will appeal only to a few fundamentalist groups. It must be admitted that the general trend over the last 25 years has been for fundamentalists to become more engaged with, and hostile towards, their perceived enemies, and less inclined to become an enclave.[8]

If the opportunity for social comparisons cannot be denied, perhaps it is possible to introduce other categories into the fundamentalist equation. The currently most favoured solution to conflict is to seek to *incorporate both the in-group and the out-group within a superordinate category*.[9] The two subordinate categories would both necessarily be salient in social situations if their members' needs and aspirations are to be met, but the distinctions between the two would decrease as a consequence of a shared superordinate identity. So, for example, evangelicals and liberals might be persuaded to internalise an Anglican or a Christian identity, in the interests of gaining more adherents. However, the prospect of al-Qaeda and the Bush administration internalising a common superordinate identity as human beings in need of peace and justice is faint indeed. Their stereotypes of modern man and terror are unlikely to break down sufficiently to permit them each to embrace the umbrella identity of human being.

Another possible conflict management strategy derived from SID is to seek to *decrease the degree of abstraction and inclusiveness of the existing comparison group*. We have already noted (see p. 34) that the more abstract and inclusive the out-group, the more extreme the in-group's prototype and stereotype, and hence the more extreme its leadership. So, when liberal Anglicans morph into 'carnality' or 'darkness' (see p. 96), the forces of spirituality and light become yet more self-righteous, and yet more Bishop Chukwumas become leaders of the Church. Reducing the size of the out-group, and making it more specific and less abstract, seems a promising strategy. So, for example, the unwillingness of several nation states to take on the role of enemy of militant Islam in a global 'war against terror' invites those militants to refine their stereotype of the whole of the rest of the world as Satan.

Another possible strategy for changing the nature of social comparison relates to *the leadership of fundamentalist movements*.

Leaders emerge partly because they are supremely prototypical. Because adherents admire these paragons of virtue and wish to be like them, they attribute charismatic leadership characteristics to them.[10] As a result of this attributed charisma, and because they accumulate some idiosyncracy credits on the way, leaders are capable of changing the BVNs of the prototype. Such changes in the prototype are likely to change the nature of the stereotype and the choice of out-group. So, for example, in the 1980s the American fundamentalist Jerry Falwell changed the prototype of American fundamentalism by making an alliance with the charismatic Pentecostals and other evangelicals. These now characterised themselves as the moral majority, and their out-group became immoral secularism.

Thus, if the fundamentalist leadership can be enticed into the rest of the world and thus compromise its stark and simple values, the prototype of their followers may be softened too. The lure of luxurious wealth and sexual opportunity proved too much for some of the moral majority's leaders, contributing to that movement's temporary eclipse. And the attraction of power, and the possibility of influencing the powerful, led to compromises in the certainties of pre-millennialist eschatological doctrine.[11] Indeed, any external bestowal of respect and status to fundamentalist leaders is likely to result in differences emerging within their movement.

There are thus various potential ways of decreasing the opportunity for social comparison with out-groups, or changing the out-groups with which comparisons are made. However, our stated aim is to *manage* fundamentalist conflict, not to *defeat* fundamentalists. All of the strategies discussed above could equally well be characterised as attempts to defeat the fundamentalist foe. This is to some extent understandable, since by 'fundamentalist conflicts' we are typically referring to situations where the fundamentalists are the prime initiators of reactionary conflict. They have acted on the basis of their overwhelming feelings of insecurity in the face of a perceived or imagined secularist assault. However, we cannot lose sight of the fact that we non-fundamentalists are also parties to the conflict. We tend to compare ourselves, as enlightened modern people, with those benighted fundamentalists. We have our stereotypes and our prototypes too.

Some of the strategies outlined above for changing social comparisons are also applicable to ourselves. For example, we may fail to differentiate between fundamentalisms, or between individual adherents of a fundamentalism. Our out-group, in other words, may be 'fundamentalism'. While fundamentalisms share five defining features, we would clearly be making a grave error if, for example, we failed to distinguish evangelical Anglicans from al-Qaeda. A common stereotype of fundamentalism would result in mistaken perceptions and inappropriate behaviour.

Changing the context

The second strategic approach to changing the conditions which favour fundamentalist conflict is to seek to change the context of social relations. The key contextual elements which are necessary conditions for inter-group conflict to occur are *insecurity* and *impermeability*.

If their security is increased, people will feel less fear and hostility. The feelings of insecurity typical of fundamentalist groups are derived from their fear that the secular world is out to destroy them. This perceived threat is treated as a cosmic war, a battle to the death. Therefore the in-group prototype is that of a warrior for God, while the out-group are the enemy. The aim is the elimination of the enemy, and the means of its achievement is the use of power. The power in question may be political power and organisation (the Anglican evangelicals), or it may be the steadfastness and faith of the Muslim vanguard (Mohammed Atta). But the focus on struggle may be decreased if the fundamentalists feel less insecure.

Likewise, if the permeability of the in-group and the out-group is increased, if they become more open to outside people and ideas, then their distinctive features will be less apparent. Depersonalisation will decrease as distinctions are blurred and as stereotypes and prototypes become less simple and stark. The cognitive conditions for conflict are less powerful.

The first and obvious contextual management strategy, then, is to nurture a feeling of greater security. Fundamentalist groups need to be persuaded that the secular world is not out to destroy them. As they are so persuaded, the nature of their out-group will change, together with their prototype and stereotype. Consequently, different leaders will emerge, since leaders tend to be those who best exemplify the prototype and least exemplify the stereotype.[12] The existing leadership will try to hang on to power, however, by continuing to emphasise the threat to the group's security, or else by choosing a new out-group which is equally threatening.

The task of persuasion is not an easy one. How can secularism and modernity be made to appear less of a threat? How can its stereotype be softened? One strategy is to increase the permeability of the groups. People and ideas from each group can make contact with each other. In particular, contact can be facilitated with those social categories which are also part of the fundamentalist's self. So, for example, 'family person' and 'American' are typically social identities which fundamentalist American Christians share with many secular modern people. The strict BVNs of fundamentalism regarding the family are likely to be at odds with, for example, the current experience of family shared by fundamentalists and non-fundamentalists alike. Fundamentalists, too, are often divorced; their children, too, are frequently wayward; and many fundamentalist wives also work away from the family home. Secularism becomes less threatening when you find that secularists have the same family issues as you.

However, fundamentalist leaders are skilled at keeping their people separate and apart.[13] Fully aware of such social realities as the state of the modern American family, they incorporate the category into the fundamentalist identity. They create nested sub-categories: Baptist single parents, for example. In this way, they manage the potentially dangerous permeability of the fundamentalist social identity. The superordinate fundamentalist BVNs subsume any divergent family BVNs, retaining the traditional fundamentalist family as the ideal while accepting deviants from it. The Christian institution of the family is being assaulted by secularists, they proclaim, and we welcome the victims of these assaults; it is not their fault that they are single parents.

Nevertheless, social, family and employment mobility, and the growth of media and communications technologies have vastly increased the probability of contact with out-group members and their BVNs. Such contact does not often by itself decrease stereotypes, however.[14] Indeed, the in-group may seek to confirm their prejudices by inducing stereotypical behaviour in the out-group when they meet them.[15] Research has clearly shown that more than just contact is usually necessary if conflict is to be reduced. The members of the two groups should be engaged in cooperative action, and with the opportunity to get to know each other as persons at more than a superficial level.[16] However, the contact need not initially be direct. For example, a fundamentalist leader could report back favourably on his own contact with an outside agency.

Such cooperative contact can soften the in-group's stereotype of the out-group, and vice versa. But it will not be effective in reducing conflict unless the in-group's social identity is retained and valued.[17] So, for example, militant Muslims might cooperate with other groups in helping to alleviate a natural disaster. But their Muslim identity has to be valued for the particular organisation it can bring to the task, or for the specific communities it can uniquely help. Any attempt to increase the permeability of a fundamentalist group by contact or involvement with other social categories has to ensure that the fundamentalist identity is not threatened, but rather is valued for what it can offer. We cannot submerge it within a superordinate category such as Christian, Muslim, Arab or the human race.

The issue obviously arises: can such management strategies hope to succeed if the fundamentalists' perceptions have more than a grain of truth in them? Clearly, many secular people do deny, and indeed ridicule, those aspects of fundamentalist belief which are most at odds with modernism, for example, belief in the supernatural causation of events. In most nation states, much social legislation permits activities which fundamentalists strongly oppose. The entertainment media do indeed spread worldwide the values of a secular modern culture. There certainly is persecution of fundamentalists in those nations where they are perceived to be a political threat. The USA and its allies do indeed engage in illegal military aggression against Arab countries. Many fundamentalists are right to feel threatened. Surely, then, identity-based strategies cannot hope to succeed unless these real-world issues are first addressed?

A social identity approach to managing fundamentalist conflict certainly does not ignore or deny those social, cultural, political and economic realities which contribute to the existence and growth of fundamentalist movements. Nor does it pretend that the management of social identity alone can hope to address the issues. Rather, I simply argue that the implications of SID have to be factored into any attempt to manage fundamentalist conflict if it is to succeed. The reality of social identity is just as real as the reality of persecution. Indeed, it is possible to construct scenarios where attempts to address the 'real' issues fail because they take no account of social identities. For example, attempts to use the media to isolate radical Muslim groups, and to distinguish them from mainstream Islam, may fail because of a failure to take account of the strength of the superordinate identity of 'Muslim' in the minds of mainstream Muslims. Or the attempt to establish western democratic institutions in Muslim nations may ignore the fact that some aspects of these institutions may violate mainstream Muslim BVNs.

Centrality of identity

The third and final condition for conflict is the degree of centrality of the fundamentalist social identity within the self of the adherent. Centrality is important because it partly *determines salience*. That is, if a social identity is of central importance and frequently used, then it is likely to be salient in the adherent's mind in a wide variety of social situations. As a consequence of salience, others within the situation are likely to be perceived in terms of this identity. They will be seen as examples of the prototype, that is a fellow member of the in-group; or as examples of a stereotype, an out-group member. Such perceptions, together with the other BVNs of the salient identity, will direct social behaviour in that situation, and make conflict more likely.

Some fundamentalists will have one completely central and dominant social identity. I have already argued (see p. 97) that Mohammed Atta and his fellow hijackers had, in effect, one social identity only: that of militant vanguard of Islam. Hence that identity will be salient in every social situation. They will be incapable of seeing the social world in any other way. Evangelical Anglicans, on the other hand, particularly laypersons, will have several prominent social identities. A social identity other than 'evangelical Christian' may consequently be salient for them in many social situations.

It is not only the centrality of the identity which will predict salience, but also the nature of the social situation. Social cues will enable the individual to judge which categories of person are present, and therefore which of his or her social identities should be salient. However, social categories are a construction of the mind. The nature of the individual's central identities will affect which other categories he or she perceives to be present. For Atta, there was only one other category: that of infidel. Individuals can construe the same social situation in markedly different ways, depending on their own different central social identities.

SID would obviously recommend the introduction of more social identities into the self if fundamentalist conflict is to be mitigated. Additional social identities could then become salient in social situations, and conflict would be less likely. I have already suggested that the increasing pace of modernisation has forced fundamentalists to make contact with, and take note of, other categories of person. However, they will only internalise these other categories as social identities if they meet *the needs for self-esteem and meaning* which their fundamentalist identities so successfully meet already.

It is important to re-emphasise this success. Fundamentalists believe themselves to be particularly chosen and favoured by God, yet at the same time they can claim credit for this favoured status in so far as they have chosen to accept and obey Him. They can feel superior to others who have not been saved, or who have not meticulously obeyed Sharia or Torah law. They have been granted knowledge which is hidden from others; indeed, they have a privileged view of history.[18] American Protestant fundamentalists have two basic narratives which encompass their entire world. Their personal world is defined by *the redemption story*, where the lost sinner is redeemed from the slavery of sin and saved by grace, confessing their sin and accepting Jesus Christ as their saviour on the basis of his atoning death on the Cross. Once saved, they are sanctified and purified, thus being prepared as witness to the world and for the salvation of souls. Their worldview is informed by *the prophecy story*, which interprets history, past present and future, as a series of supernatural divine interventions. The future is already determined, God's plan for the world having been revealed in the prophetic parts of the Bible. In sum, they have been relieved of uncertainty about what to believe, what values to hold or how to behave.

Militant Muslims, likewise, have their needs for self-esteem and meaning fully met by their BVNs. They can look forward to their reward in heaven, gaining in status as a result of their martyrdom. They, too, can look down on all others who are not militants like themselves. Their BVNs reduce any uncertainty about their social world and their place within it. They are at war, fighting for Allah, and this conflict entirely frames and informs their worldview.

Given that fundamentalists have their needs for self-esteem and meaning met so adequately by their fundamentalist social identity, why should they entertain the possibility of internalising any additional social identities? How can their apparently unshakeable belief system be loosened so as to entertain the possibility of other perspectives? One answer is to seek to raise doubts in their minds about the BVNs attached to their fundamentalist identity.

One simple method is to demonstrate that in fact *they do not share identical BVNs* with all those within the large category of which they believe themselves to be members (e.g. evangelicals). Typically, this produces the response that there are certain essentials which all in the movement share, and the rest is a matter for theological debate and interpretation. However, the task of specifying these essentials is not an easy one, and can often result in disagreement.

Moreover, there are occasions when *leaders seek to change BVNs* in order to develop the movement in new directions. Or the leadership has grown too distant from its followers, and upstart would-be leaders put forward an alternative prospectus. In both these cases, adherents necessarily have their attention drawn to the fact that BVNs are not set in stone. Once again, however, rationalisation is easily achieved in terms of the distinction between essential and optional elements. The leadership is simply adapting the movement's essential spiritual armour to better cope with the ever-changing arrows of the evil one.

A third possible opportunity to loosen up fundamentalist belief systems relates to their *basic assumptions*. Fundamentalist belief systems are usually very internally consistent. The stories they tell hang together logically, and their more formal theological statements are carefully constructed. However, the underlying assumptions are often implicit, and seldom spelled out. For example, one of the most basic assumptions is that events have supernatural causes. Either God or Satan is frequently responsible for both natural and social events (see pp. 50–53). These assumptions become explicit, however, when catastrophic events of either type occur. Two American fundamentalists were caught on tape agreeing with each other that 9/11 was God's punishment on secular America. Muslim clerics told the world on television that the tsunami disaster of 2004 demonstrated the Almighty's displeasure at the sinful lifestyle typical of tourist destinations. When basic assumptions come to the surface, and their inherent implausibility is revealed, some fundamentalists' BVNs may loosen up.

The same applies when a very specific element of the belief system is clearly *contradicted by reality*. The American Protestant, for example, is in a dilemma 'when prophecy fails' (see p. 55). When the world fails to come to an end on the date appointed, or when Christ fails to appear to rapture his followers up with him to heaven, there is some explaining to be done. Likewise, the promised victory of Allah certainly shows no signs of appearing in the foreseeable future, despite the many martyrs to the cause. Unfortunately, however, it appears that such apparent reverses only serve to increase the zeal of the faithful, being easily explained in terms of the fundamentalist belief system.

Some fundamentalists may experience a conversion into a different worldview. Any of the above ways of chipping away at fundamentalist certainties may predispose them to renounce their fundamentalism and embrace an equally powerful worldview which meets their needs for self-esteem and meaning just as well. Candidates for this new narrative might be the stories of the survival of the planet, or of the struggle for justice and peace. The provision and communication of such alternative narratives is therefore an indirect way of potentially reducing fundamentalist conflict. The postmodern denial of the possibility of any such grand narrative certainly is not.

These, however, are little more than pinpricks in the fundamentalist worldview. They can usually be rationalised away without too much difficulty, usually by reference to one of the basic assumptions (such as the inerrancy of the Bible). Perhaps yet another approach is to address the behavioural end of the BVN spectrum. Our own behaviour is often used as a way of working out what it is that we believe. I behaved in this or that way, argues the individual to him or herself, and therefore I must believe this or that.[19] There has to be some consistency between what I do and what I believe.[20] The daily activities of life in a modern society must frequently force such responses. Much of organisational life is premised on the assumption of the rational prediction and control of outcomes, rather than on supernatural intervention. Much of social life is premised on notions of social exchange and reciprocity, rather than on divinely appointed roles. Thus the very nature of modernity, and its gradual transformation into a postmodernity characterised by relativism and by mediated and individualised experience, threaten fundamentalist BVNs.

This, of course, brings us back to the basic anxiety of fundamentalisms: that secular modernity threatens to destroy them. Any explicit attempt to exploit these trends will only increase fundamentalists' reactive hostility and increase rather than mitigate conflict. Rather, the best way of addressing the conflict may be to quietly encourage and facilitate the effects of modernity and postmodernity upon fundamentalists. Their social identities may continue to provide them with self-esteem and meaning, but at the cost of increasingly flexible and individualised BVNs.

Thus in summary, SID provides several possible strategies for managing fundamentalist conflicts. The failure of those on the receiving end of fundamentalist aggression to adopt these strategies is sometimes due to their willingness to accept the role of enemy, and thus play into the fundamentalists' hands. It may also be due to their unwillingness to believe that there is nothing so practical as a good theory.

Further reading

Psychology

M.A. Hogg & D. Abrams (2003) Intergroup behaviour and social identity, in M.A. Hogg & J. Cooper (eds) *Handbook of Social Psychology*. London: Sage.

R.W. Hood, P.C. Hill & W.P. Williamson (2005) *The Psychology of Religious Fundamentalism*. New York: Guilford.

B. Spilka, R.W. Hood, B. Hunsberger & R. Gorsuch (2003) *The Psychology of Religion*, 3rd edn. New York: Guilford.

Sociology

G.A. Almond, R.S. Appleby & E. Sivan (2003) *Strong Religion: The Rise of Fundamentalisms around the World*. Chicago: University of Chicago Press.

S.F. Harding (2000) *The Book of Jerry Falwell: Fundamentalist Language and Politics*. Princeton, NJ: University of Princeton Press.

M. Juergensmeyer (2003) *Terror in the Mind of God: The Global Rise of Religious Violence*, 3rd edn. Berkeley, CA: University of California Press.

M. Lienesch (1993) *Redeeming America: Piety and Politics in the New Christian Right*. Chapel Hill, NC: University of North Carolina Press.

M. Ruthven (2004) *Fundamentalism: The Search for Meaning*. Oxford: Oxford University Press.

History

K. Armstrong (2000) *The Battle for God: Fundamentalism in Judaism, Christianity, and Islam*. London: HarperCollins.

K. Armstrong (2000) *Islam: A Short History.* London: Weidenfeld & Nicolson.

J.A. Carpenter (1997) *Revive Us Again: The Reawakening of American Fundamentalism.* New York: Oxford University Press.

Notes

Introduction

1 Princeton Religion Research Centre poll (2002) Princeton, NJ: Princeton University.
2 M. Juergensmeyer (2003) *Terror in the Mind of God: The Global Rise of Religious Violence*, 2nd edn. Berkeley, CA: University of California Press.
3 O. McTernan (2003) *Violence in God's Name: Religion in an Age of Conflict*. London: Darton, Longman, & Todd.
4 Juergensmeyer, op. cit.
5 K. Armstrong (2000) *The Battle for God: Fundamentalism in Judaism, Christianity, and Islam*. London: HarperCollins.
6 *Trends 2005*. Washington, DC: The Pew Forum.
7 C.A. Almond, R.S. Appleby & E. Sivan (2003) *Strong Religion: The Rise of Fundamentalisms around the World*. Chicago: University of Chicago Press.
8 P. Boyer (1992) *When Time Shall Be No More: Prophecy Belief in Modern American Culture*. Cambridge, MA: Harvard University Press.
9 Almond *et al.*, op. cit.
10 R.W. Hood, P.C. Hill & W.P. Williamson (2005) *The Psychology of Religious Fundamentalism*. New York: Guilford.

Chapter 1

1 G.A. Almond, R.S. Appleby & E. Sivan (2003) *Strong Religion: The Rise of Fundamentalisms around the World*, p. 17. Chicago: University of Chicago Press.
2 M. Juergensmeyer (2003) *Terror in the Mind of God: The Global Rise of Religious Violence*, 3rd edn. Berkeley, CA: University of California Press.
3 Almond *et al.*, op. cit., p. 248.
4 Ibid., p. 94.
5 K. Armstrong (2000) *Islam: A Short History*. London: Weidenfeld & Nicolson.

6 J. Carpenter (1997) *Revive Us Again: The Reawakening of American Fundamentalism.* Oxford: Oxford University Press.
7 M. Lienesch (1993) *Redeeming America: Piety and Politics in the New Christian Right.* Chapel Hill, NC: University of North Carolina Press.
8 Juergensmeyer, op. cit.
9 S. Bates (2004) *A Church at War: Anglicans and Homosexuality.* London: I.B.Tauris.
10 Almond *et al.*, op. cit.
11 S.P. Huntington (1995) *The Clash of Civilisations and the Remaking of World Order.* New York: Simon & Schuster.
12 Almond *et al.*, op. cit.
13 K. Armstrong (2000) *The Battle for God: Fundamentalism in Judaism, Christianity and Islam.* London: HarperCollins.
14 S. Bruce (2000) *Fundamentalism.* Cambridge: Polity Press.
15 Almond *et al.*, op. cit., p. 124.
16 Armstrong, op. cit.
17 Lienesch, op. cit.
18 P. Boyer (1992) *When Time Shall Be No More: Prophecy Belief in Modern American Culture.* Cambridge, MA: Harvard University Press.
19 Armstrong, op. cit.
20 W.C. Roof (1999) *Spiritual Marketplace: Baby Boomers and the Remaking of American Religion.* Princeton, NJ: Princeton University Press.
21 P.A. Tickle (1998) *God-talk in America.* New York: Crossroad.
22 Juergensmeyer, op. cit.
23 www.youngmuslims.ca.
24 Bates, op. cit.
25 M. Durham (2000) *The Christian Right, the Far Right, and the Boundaries of American Conservatism.* Manchester: Manchester University Press.
26 R. Balmer (1999) *Mine Eyes Have Seen the Glory: A Journey into the Evangelical Subculture in America,* 3rd edn, pp. 147 ff. New York: Oxford University Press.
27 Bruce, op. cit.
28 Armstrong, op. cit.
29 Carpenter, op. cit.
30 Juergensmeyer, op. cit., p. 174.
31 Ibid., p. 150.
32 O. McTernan (2003) *Violence in God's Name: Religion in an Age of Conflict.* London: Darton, Oliver & Todd.
33 Almond *et al.*, op. cit., p. 96.
34 Lienesch, op. cit.
35 L. Festinger (1957) *A Theory of Cognitive Dissonance.* New York: Row Peterson.
36 *The Chicago Statement on Biblical Inerrancy* (1978) Chicago: International Council on Biblical Inerrancy. Obtainable from The Coalition on Revival, Inc., P.O.Box A, Sunnyvale, California 94087, USA.
37 R.W. Hood, P.C. Hill & W.P. Williamson (2005) *The Psychology of Religious Fundamentalism.* New York: Guilford.

38 C. Van Til (1967) *The Defence of the Faith*. Phillipsburg, NJ: Presbyterian and Reformed Publishing Co.
39 Almond *et al.*, op. cit. p. 144.
40 Ibid., p. 135.
41 Lienesch, op. cit.
42 S.F. Harding (2000) *The Book of Jerry Falwell: Fundamentalist Language and Politics*. Princeton, NJ: Princeton University Press.
43 Boyer, op. cit.

Chapter 2

1 D. Fontana (2003) *Psychology, Religion, and Spirituality*. Oxford: BPS Blackwell.
2 B. Spilka, R.W. Hood, B.Hunsberger & R.Gorsuch (2003) *The Psychology of Religion*, 3rd edn. New York: Guilford.
3 Spilka *et al.*, op. cit., p. 390.
4 M.A. Hogg & D. Abrams (2003) Intergroup behaviour and social identity, in M.A.Hogg & J.Cooper (eds) *Handbook of Social Psychology*. London: Sage.
5 M.A. Hogg & D.J. Terry (2001) Social identity theory and organisational processes, in M.A. Hogg & D.J.Terry (eds) *Social Identity Processes in Organisational Contexts*. Philadelphia, PA: Psychology Press.
6 M.A. Hogg (2003) Social identity, in M.R. Leary & J.P. Tangney (eds) *Handbook of Self and Identity*. New York: Guilford.
7 M.A. Hogg & D. Abrams (2001) Inter-group relations: an overview, in M.A. Hogg & D. Abrams (eds) *Inter-group Relations: Essential Readings*. Philadelphia, PA: Psychology Press.
8 Hogg & Abrams (2003) op. cit., p. 412.
9 H.C. Triandis (1995) *Individualism and Collectivism*. Boulder, CO: Westview Press.
10 G. Hofstede (1980) *Culture's Consequences*. Beverley Hills, CA: Sage.
11 H. Tajfel (ed.) (1978) *Differentiation Between Social Groups: Studies in the Social Psychology of Inter-group Relations*. London: Academic Press.
12 W. Doise *et al.* (1972) An experimental investigation into the formation of intergroup representations, *European Journal of Social Psychology*, 2: 202–4.
13 H. Tajfel & J.C. Turner (1979) An integrative theory of intergroup conflict, in W.G. Austin & S. Worchel (eds) *The Social Psychology of Intergroup Relations*. Monterey, CA: Brooks Cole.
14 R.F. Baumeister (1999) The nature and structure of the self: an overview, in R.F.Baumeister (ed.) *The Self in Social Psychology*. Philadelphia, PA: Psychology Press.
15 J.C. Turner (1982) Towards a cognitive redefinition of the social group, in H. Tajfel (ed.) *Social Identity and Intergroup Relations*. Cambridge: Cambridge University Press.
16 D.H. Watt (2002) *Bible-carrying Christians*. New York: Oxford University Press.

17 M. Lienesch (1993) *Redeeming America: Piety and Politics in the New Christian Right.* Chapel Hill, NC: University of North Carolina Press.
18 J.C. Turner (1985) Social categorisation and the self-concept: a social cognitive theory of group behaviour, in E.J. Lawler (ed.) *Advances in Group Processes,* vol. 2. Greenwich, CT: JAI Press.
19 S.A. Haslam, & N. Ellemers (2005) Social identity in industrial and organisational psychology: concepts, controversies, and contributions, in G.P. Hodgkinson (ed.) *International Review of Industrial and Organisational Psychology,* vol. 20. Chichester: Wiley.
20 Turner (1982), op. cit.
21 S.F. Harding (2000) *The Book of Jerry Falwell: Fundamentalist Language and Politics.* Princeton, NJ: Princeton University Press.
22 P.A.Tickle (1997) *God-talk in America.* New York: Crossroad.
23 Lienesch, op. cit.
24 Harding, op. cit.
25 S.A. Haslam (2001) *Psychology in Organisations: The Social Identity Approach,* p. 64. London: Sage.
26 S.A. Haslam *et al.* (1995) Contextual shifts in the prototypicality of extreme and moderate outgroup members, *European Journal of Social Psychology,* 25: 509–30.
27 Hogg & Abrams (2003), op. cit., p. 416.
28 Tajfel, op. cit.
29 Hogg & Abrams (2003), op. cit., p. 414.
30 N. Ellemers *et al.* (1992) Status protection in high status minority groups, *European Journal of Social Psychology,* 22: 123–40.
31 M.A. Hogg & D. Abrams (1988) *Social Identifications: A Social Psychology of Intergroup Relations and Social Processes.* London: Routledge.
32 B. Doosje, N. Ellemers & R. Spears (1995) Perceived intragroup variability as a function of group status and identification, *Journal of Experimental Social Psychology,* 31, 410-36.
33 N. Ellemers, R. Spears & B. Doosje (1997) Sticking together or falling apart: in-group identification as a psychological determinant of group commitment versus individual mobility, *Journal of Personality and Social Psychology,* 72: 617–26.
34 R. Spears, B. Doosje & N. Ellemers (1997) Self-stereotyping in the face of threats to group status and distinctiveness: the role of group indentification, *Personality and Social Psychology Bulletin,* 23: 538–53.
35 N. Ellemers, P. Kortekaas & J. Ouwerkerk (1999) Self-categorisation, commitment to the group, and group self-esteem as related but distinct aspects of social identity, *European Journal of Social Psychology,* 29: 371–89.
36 M.A. Hogg & B.A. Mullin (1999) Joining groups to reduce uncertainty: subjective uncertainty reduction and group identification, in D. Abrams & M.A. Hogg (eds.) *Social Identity and Social Cognition.* Oxford: Blackwell.
37 P. Boyer (1992) *When Time Shall Be No More: Prophecy Belief in Modern American Culture.* Cambridge, MA: Harvard University Press.
38 K.A. Quinn, C.N. Macrae & G.V. Bodenhausen (2003) Stereotyping and impression formation: how categorical thinking shapes person

perception, in M.A. Hogg & J. Cooper (eds) *Handbook of Social Psychology*. London: Sage.
39 R.Balmer (2000) *Mine Eyes Have Seen the Glory: A Journey into the Evangelical Subculture in America*, 3rd edn, pp. 226 ff. New York: Oxford University Press.
40 Hogg & Abrams (2003), op. cit., p. 414.
41 Hogg & Mullin, op. cit., p. 269.
42 Haslam, op. cit., p. 56.

Chapter 3

1 L. Kellstedt & C. Smidt (1991) Measuring fundamentalism: an analysis of different operational strategies, *Journal for the Scientific Study of Religion*, 30: 259–78.
2 P.C. Hill & R.W. Hood (1999) *Measures of Religiosity*. Birmingham, AL: Religious Education Press.
3 B. Altemeyer & B. Hunsberger (1992) Authoritarianism, religious fundamentalism, quest, and prejudice, *International Journal of the Psychology of Religion*, 2: 113–33.
4 L.M. Jackson & B. Hunsberger (1999) An intergroup perspective on religion and prejudice, *Journal for the Scientific Study of Religion*, 38: 509–23.
5 A.W. Eister (1973) H. Reinhold Niebuhr and the paradox of religious organisations: a radical critique, in C.Y. Glock & P.E. Hammond (eds) *Beyond the Classics? Essays in the Scientific Study of Religion*. New York: Harper & Row.
6 R. Stark (1985) Church and sect, in P.E. Hammond (ed.) *The Sacred in a Secular Age*. Berkeley, CA: University of California Press.
7 R. Finke & R. Stark (2001) The new holy clubs: testing church-to-sect propositions, *Sociology of Religion*, 62: 175–89.
8 W.S. Bainbridge & R. Stark (1980) Sectarian tension, *Review of Religious Research*, 22: 105–24.
9 www.publiceye.org/apocalyptic.
10 B. Johnson (1993) The denominations: the changing map of religious America, in Roper Centre, *The Public Perspective*. Storrs, CT: University of Connecticut Press.
11 D.M. Kelley (1972) *Why Conservative Churches are Growing*. New York: Harper & Row.
12 L. Iannacone (1994) Why strict churches are strong, *American Journal of Sociology*, 99: 1180–211.
13 D.V.A. Olson & P. Perl (2001) Variations in strictness and religious commitment among five denominations, *Journal for the Scientific Study of Religion*, 40: 757–64.
14 M. Hout, A. Greely & M.J. Wilde (2001) The demographic imperative in religious change in the United States, *American Journal of Sociology*, 107: 468–500.
15 R. Stark & R. Finke (2000) *Acts of Faith: Explaining the Human Side of Religion*. Berkeley, CA: University of California Press.

16 J.Z. Park & S.H. Reimer (2002) Revisiting the social sources of American Christianity, 1972–1998, *Journal for the Scientific Study of Religion*, 41: 733–46.

17 J.B. Tamney *et al.* (2003) Strictness and congregational growth in Middletown, *Journal for the Scientific Study of Religion*, 42: 363–75.

18 M. Ostow (1990) The fundamentalist phenomenon: a psychological perspective, in N.J. Cohen (ed.) *The Fundamentalist Phenomenon*. Grand Rapids, MI: Eerdmans.

19 K.A. Quinn, C.N. Macrae & G.V. Bodenhausen (2003) Stereotyping and impression formation: how categorical thinking shapes person perception, in M.A. Hogg & J. Cooper (eds) *Handbook of Social Psychology*. London: Sage.

20 B. Hunsberger (1996) Religious fundamentalism, right-wing authoritarianism, and hostility in non-Christian religious groups, *International Journal of the Psychology of Religion*, 6: 39–49.

21 L.A. Kirkpatrick, R.W. Hood & G. Hartz (1991) Fundamentalist religion conceptualised in terms of Rokeach's theory of the open and closed mind: new perspectives on some old ideas, *Research in the Social Scientific Study of Religion*, 3: 157–70.

22 B. Altemeyer (1988) *Enemies of Freedom: Understanding Right-wing Authoritarianism*. San Francisco: Jossey-Bass.

23 B. Altemeyer (1996) *The Authoritarian Spectre*. Boston, MA: Harvard University Press.

24 T.W. Adorno *et al.* (1950) *The Authoritarian Personality*. New York: Harper & Row.

25 B. Altemeyer & B. Hunsberger (1992) Authoritarianism, religious fundamentalism, quest, and prejudice, *International Journal of the Psychology of Religion*, 2: 113–33.

26 B. Laythe, D.G. Finkel & L.A. Kirkpatrick (2001) Predicting prejudice from religious fundamentalism and right-wing authoritarianism: a multiple-regression approach, *Journal for the Scientific Study of Religion*, 40: 1–10.

27 B. Laythe *et al.* (2002) Religious fundamentalism as a predictor of prejudice: a two-component model, *Journal for the Scientific Study of Religion*, 41: 623–35.

28 Jackson & Hunsberger, op. cit.

29 L.A. Kirkpatrick (1993) Fundamentalism, Christian orthodoxy, and intrinsic religious orientation as predictors of discriminatory attitudes, *Journal for the Scientific Study of Religion*, 32: 256–68.

30 C.D. Batson, P. Schoenrade & W.L. Ventis, (1993) *Religion and the Individual*. New York: Oxford University Press.

31 S. Bates (2004) *A Church at War: Anglicans and Homosexuality*. London: I.B.Tauris.

32 C. Van Til (1976) *The Defence of the Faith*. Philadelphia, PA: Presbyterian and Reformed Publishing Co.

33 A.S. Fulton, R.L. Gorsuch & E.A. Maynard (1999) Religious orientation, anti-homosexual sentiment, and fundamentalism among Christians, *Journal for the Scientific Study of Religion*, 38: 14–22.

34 B. Spilka *et al.* (2003) *The Psychology of Religion*, 3rd edn. New York: Guilford.
35 D.M. Wulff (1997) *Psychology of Religion: Classic and Contemporary Views*, 2nd edn. New York: Wiley.
36 M. Lienesch (1993) *Redeeming America: Piety and Politics in the New Christian Right*. Chapel Hill, NC: University of North Carolina Press.
37 P. Boyer (1992) *When Time Shall Be No More: Prophecy Belief in Modern American Culture*. Cambridge, MA: Harvard University Press.
38 B. Spilka, P. Shaver & L.A. Kirkpatrick (1983) A general attribution theory for the psychology of religion, *Journal for the Scientific Study of Religion*, 24: 1–20.
39 S. Johnson & B. Spilka (1991) Religion and the breast cancer patient: the roles of clergy and faith, *Journal of Religion and Health*, 30: 21–33.
40 M.P. Lupfer, K.F. Brock & S.J. DePaola (1992) The use of secular and religious attributions to explain everyday behaviour, *Journal for the Scientific Study of Religion*, 31: 486–503.
41 R.L. Gorsuch & C.S. Smith (1983) Attributions of responsibility to God: an interaction of religious beliefs and outcomes, *Journal for the Scientific Study of Religion*, 22: 340–52.
42 B. Spilka & G. Schmidt (1983) General attribution theory for the study of religion: the influence of event-character on attributions to God, *Journal for the Scientific Study of Religion*, 22: 326–39.
43 M.H. Miner & J. McKnight (1999) Religious attributions: situational factors and effects in coping, *Journal for the Scientific Study of Religion*, 38: 274–86.
44 M. Weeks & M.B. Lupfer (2000) Religious attributions and proximity of influence: an investigation of direct interventions and distal explanations, *Journal for the Scientific Study of Religion*, 39: 348–62.
45 G.L. Bahnsen (1991) *No Other Standard*. Tyler, TX: Institute for Christian Economics.
46 K.I. Pargament *et al.* (1988) Religion and the problem-solving process: three styles of coping, *Journal for the Scientific Study of Religion*, 27: 90–104.
47 J.B. Kenworthy (2003) Explaining the belief in God for self, in-group, and out-group targets, *Journal for the Scientific Study of Religion*, 42: 137–46.
48 R.W. Hood (1992) Sin and guilt in faith traditions: issues for self-esteem, in J.F. Schumaker (ed.) *Religion and Mental Health*. New York: Oxford University Press.
49 W.C. Rowatt *et al.* (2002) On being holier-than-thou or humbler-than-thee: a social psychological perspective on religiousness and humility, *Journal for the Scientific Study of Religion*, 41: 227–37.
50 B. Hunsberger, M. Pratt & S. Pancer (1994) Religious fundamentalism and integrative complexity of thought: a relationship for existential content only? *Journal for the Scientific Study of Religion*, 33: 335–46.
51 S.M. Pancer *et al.* (1995) Religious orthodoxy and the complexity of thought about religious and non-religious issues, *Journal of Personality*, 63: 213–32.
52 Hunsberger *et al.*, op.cit., p. 2.

53 B. Hunsberger *et al.* (1996) Religious fundamentalism and religious doubts: content, connections, and complexity of thinking, *International Journal of the Psychology of Religion*, 6: 201–20.
54 B. Altemeyer & B. Hunsberger (1997) *Amazing Conversions: Why Some Turn to Faith, and Others Abandon Religion.* Amherst, NY: Prometheus Books.
55 S. McFarland & J. Warren (1992) Religious orientations and selective exposure among fundamentalist Christians, *Journal for the Scientific Study of Religion*, 31: 163–74.
56 L. Festinger, H.W. Riecken & S. Schachter (1956) *When Prophecy Fails.* Minneapolis, MN: University of Minnesota Press.
57 C. Bader (1999) New perspectives on failed prophecy, *Journal for the Scientific Study of Religion*, 39: 119–31.
58 S. Dein (2001) What really happens when prophecy fails: the case of Lubavitch, *Sociology of Religion*, 62: 383–401.

Chapter 4

1 www.werismyki.com/articles/atta.
2 *The Observer*, 6 September, 2003.
3 B. Lincoln (2002) *Holy Terrors: Thinking about Religion after September 11.* Chicago: University of Chicago Press.
4 G.A. Almond, R.S. Appleby & E. Sivan (2003) *Strong Religion: The Rise of Fundamentalisms around the World.* Chicago: University of Chicago Press.
5 Qur'ān, 9: 4.
6 M. Juergensmeyer (2000) *Terror in the Mind of God: The Global Rise of Religious Violence.* Berkeley, CA: University of California Press.
7 K. Armstrong (2000) *Islam: A Short History.* London: Weidenfeld & Nicolson.
8 Almond *et al.*, op. cit., p. 248.
9 P. Boyer (1992) *When Time Shall Be No More: Prophecy Belief in Modern American Culture.* Cambridge, MA: Harvard University Press.
10 *Los Angeles Times*, 27 January, 2002.
11 *The Observer*, 23 September, 2001.
12 *The Observer*, 20 June, 2004.
13 www.nmhschool.org/tthornton/sayyid_abu.htm.
14 K. Armstrong (2000) *The Battle for God: Fundamentalism in Judaism, Christianity, and Islam.* London: HarperCollins.
15 S.A.A. Mawdudi (1976) *Jihad in Islam*, p. 28. Lahore: Islamic Publications.
16 S. Qutb (1981) *Milestones*, Ch. 4. New Delhi: Markazi Maktaba Islami.
17 Qutb, ibid., Ch. 4.
18 Qutb, ibid., Ch. 5.
19 Qutb, ibid., Ch. 5.
20 Qur'ān, 13:139.
21 Qutb, op. cit., Ch. 11.
22 S. Qutb (1968) *The America I Have Seen*, quoted on www.npr.org/templates/story/story.php?storyId=1253796.

23 Qutb, op. cit., Ch. 11.
24 Qutb, ibid., Ch. 11.
25 S.F. Harding (2000)*The Book of Jerry Falwell: Fundamentalist Language and Politics*. Princeton, NJ: Princeton University Press.
26 Juergensmeyer, op. cit.
27 P.A. Tickle (1997) *God-talk in America*, p. 189. New York: Crossroad.
28 R. Woodward (2002) *Bush at War*. New York: Simon & Schuster.
29 B. Barron (1992) *Heaven on Earth? The Social and Political Agendas of Dominion Theology*. Grand Rapids, MI: Zondervan.
30 G. Kepel (2004) *The War for Muslim Minds: Islam and the West*. Cambridge, MA: Bellknap Press.

Chapter 5

1 M. Furlong (2000) *C of E: The State It's In*. London: Hodder & Stoughton.
2 G.A. Almond, R.S. Appleby & E. Sivan (2003) *Strong Religion: The Rise of Fundamentalisms around the World*. Chicago: University of Chicago Press.
3 Princeton Religion Research Centre poll (2002) Princeton University, Princeton, NJ.
4 S. Bates (2004) *A Church at War: Anglicans and Homosexuality*. London: I.B. Tauris.
5 Furlong, op. cit., pp. 326 ff.
6 Bates, op. cit., p. 7.
7 Bates, ibid., p. 105.
8 *Issues in Human Sexuality: A Statement to the House of Bishops* (1991) London: Church House Publishing.
9 Bates, op. cit., p. 139.
10 Bates, ibid., p. 145.
11 Bates, ibid., pp. 157 ff.
12 Bates, ibid., pp. 155 ff.
13 Bates, ibid., pp. 180 ff.
14 Bates, ibid., pp. 200 ff.
15 *The Guardian*, 19 October, 2004.
16 *The Guardian*, 17 November, 2005.
17 R.J. Fisher (2000) Inter-group conflict, in M. Deutsch & P.T. Coleman (eds) *The Handbook of Conflict Resolution*. San Francisco: Jossey-Bass.
18 C. Hardy & S.R. Clegg (1996) Some dare call it power, in S.R. Clegg, C. Hardy & W.R. Nord (eds) *Handbook of Organisational Studies*. London: Sage.
19 Furlong, op. cit., pp. 234 ff.
20 Bates, op. cit., p. 13.
21 Bates, ibid., p. 24.
22 Bates ibid., pp. 130 ff.
23 *New York Times*, 22 May, 2004.
24 Bates, op. cit., p. 132.

25 Bates, ibid., p. 96.
26 Hardy & Clegg, op. cit.
27 Bates, op. cit., pp. 148 ff.
28 Bates, ibid., p. 150.
29 Bates, ibid., p. 164.
30 Bates, ibid., p. 163.
31 Bates, ibid., p. 192.
32 Bates, ibid., pp. 197 ff.
33 Bates, ibid., p. 222.
34 Bates, ibid., p. 227.
35 Bates, ibid., pp. 136–7.
36 Bates, ibid., p. 23.
37 Bates, ibid., p. 139.
38 Bates, ibid., p. 22.
39 Bates, ibid., p. 23.
40 Bates, ibid., p. 17.

Chapter 6

1 S.F. Harding (2000) *The Book of Jerry Falwell: Fundamentalist Language and Politics*. Princeton, NJ: Princeton University Press.
2 www.observer.guardian.co.uk/international/story/0,6903,560773,00. html.
3 S. Bates (2004) *A Church at War: Anglicans and Homosexuality*. London: I.B. Tauris.
4 Bates, ibid., p. 195.
5 www.observer.guardian.co.uk/waronterrorism/story/0,1373,556630,00. html.
6 www.marty-center.uchicago.edu/webforum/122002/commentary.shtml.
7 Bates, op. cit., p. 29.
8 C. Smith (2000) *Christian America? What Evangelicals Really Want*. Berkeley, CA: University of California Press.
9 Bates, op. cit., p. 16.
10 B. Lincoln (2002) *Holy Terrors: Thinking about Religion after September 11*. Chicago: University of Chicago Press.
11 Lincoln, ibid.
12 Bates, op. cit., p. 23.
13 Bates, ibid., p. 29.
14 S.A. Haslam & S.D. Reicher (2005) The psychology of tyranny, *Scientific American Mind*, 16(3): 44–51.
15 Frances Jane van Alstyne (1820–1915) (1906), in I.D.Sankey (ed.) *Sacred Songs and Solos*. London: Morgan & Scott.
16 The Bible, Leviticus, 18:22, 20:13.
17 The Bible, I Corinthians, 6:9–10.
18 Bates, op. cit., p. 10.
19 S. Qutb (1981) *Milestones*, Ch. 5. New Delhi: Markazi Maktaba Islami.
20 Smith, op. cit.
21 Qutb, op. cit.

22 M. Juergensmeyer (2003) *Terror in the Mind of God: The Global Rise of Religious Violence*, 3rd edn. Berkeley, CA: University of California Press.
23 O. McTernan (2003) *Violence in God's Name: Religion in an Age of Conflict*. London: Darton, Longman, & Todd.

Chapter 7

1 T.F. Pettigrew (1998) Intergroup contact theory, *Annual Review of Psychology*, 49: 65–85.
2 R.J. Fisher (2000) Intergroup conflict, in M. Deutsch & P.T. Coleman (eds) *Handbook of Conflict Resolution*. San Francisco: Jossey-Bass.
3 Fisher, ibid., p. 179.
4 M. Deutsch (1973) *The Resolution of Conflict: Constructive and Destructive Processes*. New Haven, CT: Yale University Press.
5 B.B. Bunker (2000) Managing conflict through large group methods, in M. Deutsch & P.T.Coleman (eds) *Handbook of Conflict Resolution*. San Francisco: Jossey-Bass.
6 S. Bates (2004) *A Church at War: Anglicans and Homosexuality*, p. 190. London: I.B.Tauris.
7 M.A. Hogg (2001) Social identification, group prototypicality, and emergent leadership, in M.A. Hogg & D.J. Terry (eds) *Social Identity Processes in Organisational Contexts*. Philadelphia, PA: Psychology Press.
8 G.A. Almond, R.S. Appleby & E. Sivan (2003) *Strong Religion: The Rise of Fundamentalisms around the World*, pp. 23 ff. Chicago: University of Chicago Press.
9 S.L. Gaertner & J.F. Dovidio (2000) *Reducing Intergroup Bias: The Common Ingroup Identity Model*. Philadelphia, PA: Psychology Press.
10 Hogg, op. cit.
11 P. Boyer (1992) *When Time Shall Be No More: Prophecy Belief in Modern American Culture*. Cambridge, MA: Harvard University Press.
12 Hogg, op. cit., p. 204.
13 Almond *et al.*, op. cit.
14 M. Snyder (1992) Motivational foundations of behavioural confirmation, in M.P. Zanna (ed.) *Advances in Experimental Social Psychology*, vol. 25. San Diego, CA: Academic Press.
15 T.F. Pettigrew & L.R. Tropp (2000) Does intergroup contact reduce prejudice? Recent meta-analytic findings, in S. Oskamp (ed.) *Reducing Prejudice and Discrimination*. Mahwah, NJ: Lawrence Erlbaum Associates, Inc.
16 Gaertner & Dovidio, op. cit.
17 Boyer, op. cit.
18 Boyer, ibid.
19 D.J. Bem (1972) Self-perception theory, in L. Berkowitz (ed.) *Advances in Experimental Social Psychology*, vol. 6. New York: Academic Press.
20 L. Festinger (1957) *A Theory of Cognitive Dissonance*. Evanston, IL: Row Peterson.

Index